PURSUING THE WILL OF GOD

Reflections and Meditations

PURSUING THE WILL OF GOD

Reflections and Meditations on the Life of Abraham

JACK HAYFORD

Living Way Ministries ®
Van Nuys, California, 91405-2233

PURSUING THE WILL OF GOD
published by Living Way Ministries

International Standard Book Number: 0-916847-35-7

Cover design by Michelle Glush

Printed in Colombia
by Editorial Buena Semilla

FOR INFORMATION:
Living Way Ministries ®
14800 Sherman Way, Van Nuys, California, 91405-2233
818-779-8400 • www.livingway.org

Library of Congress Cataloging-in-Publication Data
Hayford, Jack W
Pursuing the Will of God: Reflections and Meditations on the Life of Abraham
by Jack Hayford. p.cm. *ISBN 0-916847-35-7*
1. Abraham (Biblical patriarch)—Meditations. 2. Christian life—Meditations.
3. God—Will—Meditations. I. Title

Contents

CHAPTER ONE

The Commitment to God's Will

Two small, almost inconspicuous objects rest on the mantle of our home. And they have a world of meaning for me.

When I placed them there years ago, I pictured people coming into our living room, seeing them, and asking about them. Then (as I imagined it), I would casually lean back against the mantle and tell them the story behind those objects.

Trouble is, no one has ever asked.

So I've come to realize over the years that they are there for me...to remind me of a principle that reaches back more than forty-five years into my personal history.

The two objects are a mortar and a pestle.

Together, these items have come to symbolize the trade of the pharmacist and the apothecary shop. The mortar is a little mixing bowl, and the pestle is a rounded rod used to grind up substances into powders—the ingredients of a particular prescription. The mixing, of course, is carefully done. It is precise. It is purposeful. And the result is potent! It brings life and healing.

When I was in high school, I had my eyes set on being a pharmicist. The teachers and counselors had high expectations for young Jack Hayford, one of the top students in his class at Tech High in Oakland, California. And I didn't intend to disappoint them! With their encouragement, I had pretty well established the course of my life. My neatly constructed plans called for me to graduate from Tech, then enter the School of Pharmacy at the University of California in Berkeley.

I could see my life stretching out before me. I was quite sure at that point that I was going to spend my working life in a spotless white smock behind a pharmacy counter, quietly mixing and dispensing medicines. It seemed obvious and natural. A comfortable, secure life.

Then, in one evening, *everything* changed.

I suddenly found myself at an unexpected crossroads in my life—and things didn't look quite so pat and secure anymore! It happened at a youth conference at (of all places) the *Berkeley* Presbyterian Church. When the speaker that night gave the appeal for those who would surrender everything about their lives to the Lord, I purposefully stood and walked to the front of the auditorium. And just like that, my life plans changed forever.

Walking down the aisle at that meeting was no whim. My response to the Lord that night was an echo of an experience eight years earlier—a memory that came flooding back to me with piercing clarity at that youth rally. I was eight years old when the Lord first told me what *His* purpose was for my life. I'd wrestled with that knowledge as a child, never saying a word about it to anybody in the subsequent eight years.

But now, at the age of sixteen, I was hearing the Lord again. And there was no mistaking His words in my heart: *Son...your life is not your own.*

This time I heeded His words. I obeyed His call. And the whole course of my life began flowing in a new channel, a new direction.

The mortar and pestle on the mantle? They're the classic tools of the pharmacist's trade—representing the purposes *I* had planned. But now, they're a reminder to me that it's infinitely wiser to "let the Lord mix the prescription for your life." Rather than concocting your own ingredients and formulating your own schemes, if you leave the planning to Him, your days will be richer in meaning and purpose.

On reflection, I would guess that at least half of my private conversations with brothers and sisters in Christ—people who love the Lord Jesus and truly desire to please Him—concern the outworking of God's will in their personal lives.

As you read this book, I believe the Holy Spirit will teach you—or perhaps remind you once again—of some enduring fundamentals in the life of faith. And the first one is simply this...

Let the Lord write the prescription for your life.

Let Him mix the ingredients.

Let Him write the instructions.

Don't presume to direct your own life on your own terms. Discovering the will of your Creator and Savior—and walking in that will—may not be the most "secure" way to live, according to the world's standards. But I assure you of this: It will be the most fulfilling thing that could ever happen to you.

YOUR PLACE IN HIS WILL

Now the LORD had said to Abram:
"Get out of your country,
From your family
And from your father's house,
To a land that I will show you.
I will make you a great nation;
I will bless you
And make your name great;
And you shall be a blessing.
I will bless those who bless you,
And I will curse him who curses you;
And in you all the families of the earth
shall be blessed."

> So Abram departed as the LORD had spoken to him, and Lot went with him. And Abram was seventy-five years old when he departed from Haran. (Genesis 12:1–4)

Some of us have the idea that pursuing the will of God is chiefly a concern of young people. We may look at those in the under-thirty age bracket—teens, college students, young couples—and find ourselves thinking, "Ah well, the future lies with them. It's like you said, Jack. The Lord called you at age eight and confirmed it at age sixteen. He's looking for young people, with their lives still before them."

Yet isn't it interesting? When God reached down in His grace and picked out a man who would become the very model of "walking by faith" for all generations to follow, He selected a man who was *seventy-five years old*. God certainly could have tapped Abraham[1] on the shoulder when he was twenty-five, thirty-five, or forty-five. But He waited until the man from Ur was a seasoned elder, pushing eighty.

It wasn't the last time He'd do such a thing.

Moses became the leader of a nation at eighty.

Caleb hitched up his britches and led a major military offensive against a determined foe at eighty-five.

Haggai the prophet was at least ninety when he delivered his powerful prophetic message about rebuilding the temple following the Babylonian exile. His words had a ring of authority about them because Haggai had been on the scene more than seventy years earlier, before the old temple was destroyed. His exhortation carried weight because he'd experienced so much.

Simeon enters the pages of Bible history near the very end of his days. He was granted the unspeakable honor of cradling the infant Son of God in his arms, as he prophesied the rising and falling of nations and future salvation for the Gentiles—you and me.

It's possible that the Lord will one day bring an authority of years to you too—a stability, a maturity that will make you a unique and well-honed instrument in His hands.

Don't get me wrong though; there is ample place for the young in God's scheme of things. Within Jesus' own band of disciples, it's likely there was at least one teenager: John was probably seventeen or eighteen when he began following the Lord. And possibly at least half the disciples were under thirty or very near that age.

So here's the bottom line: *There's a place in God's will for you, no matter what your age, no matter what your past.* The prophet Joel wrote: "I will pour out My Spirit on all flesh; your sons and your daughters shall prophesy, your old men shall dream dreams, your young men shall see visions" (Joel 2:28). In the course of my ministry, I have seen all of these things happen!

So don't ever write yourself out of the program of God.

Don't ever assume God's will is "for someone else."

Don't ever suppose He's finished with you or "set you aside."

Listen, if He were *finished* with you, He'd take you home! If you're here on the planet and still breathing, He has something for you to do and to be. And the power of His Spirit can make it happen. Don't presume to remove yourself from the *development* of His will in your life simply because of who you are, how old you are, or your phase of life. (Remember, just before he received the biggest commission of his life, Moses thought of himself as a stammering, elderly has-been!)

About the time we reach our middle years, we have a tendency to begin thinking, "Well, life is passing me by. My course is pretty well set. I'm running along this railroad track, and now it's just a matter of riding it out."

Friend...*how do you know?*

How do you know what God has planned for you? How can you or I possibly predict what doors of opportunity or service He might throw open for us in the next year, the next month, or even *tomorrow?* Is anything too hard for Him? Is He limited by your perceived weakness or inadequacies? Is He intimidated by your less-than-stellar track record? You and I have a responsibility to pursue the will of God every day of our lives, wherever we are in our life's journey. *The Lord is wanting to say something to you now—at your age, where you are this week, this day, this period in your life—about His will for you.*

Are you seeking His voice? Are you pursuing His will full heartedly?

DON'T PULL UP SHORT OF GOD'S DESTINATION FOR YOU

> Terah took his son Abram and his grandson Lot, the son of Haran, and his daughter-in-law, Sarai, his son Abram's wife, and they went out with them from Ur of the Chaldeans to go to the land of Canaan; and they came to Haran and dwelt there. So the days of Terah were two hundred and five years, and Terah died in Haran. (Genesis 11:31–32)

It was a great start.

God had called Abraham while he was still in Mesopotamia, before he ever came to Haran, to go to a land God would show him (see Acts 7:2–3). So Abraham, his father, Terah, his wife, Sarah, and his nephew, Lot, pulled up stakes and left their ancestral home in Ur of the Chaldeans.

If you could get into Iraq, you could view the ruins of Ur today. It's about eight hundred miles from the land that would become Israel. Archaeologists have uncovered the remains of a remarkably developed civilization on that site. This wasn't some fly-by-night band of Bedouins who simply folded up their tents, threw their stuff on a couple of camels, and went plodding off across the desert. Abraham and his family were leaving a scene of success, prosperity, sophistication, science, and learning. What kind of home had they abandoned on the banks of the Euphrates? How many relatives and friends and neighbors had they left behind? What kind of business deals did Abraham have to walk away from? Did Sarah give up teaching harp lessons on Tuesday and Thursday evenings?

The Bible doesn't say. It simply tells us that "they went out...from Ur of the Chaldeans to go to the land of Canaan."

It truly was a commendable beginning. After all, the hardest part of such a journey might very well be cutting loose and traveling those first ten miles. Gradually they leave the familiar, bustling streets of Ur behind, making their way through the gracious and well-appointed suburbs. Then they're at the outskirts of the city, and then...the city is behind them. As they travel yet further down the road, the last few dwellings thin out, the traffic dwindles, the grazing livestock becomes sparse, and then—at last—Ur is truly, finally, out of sight.

Forever? When you're only one day's journey away, the temptation is still there to turn around...to change your mind...to head back...to go home...to reach back for the familiar and the secure...to look back, as Lot's own wife would do one day. But Abraham's family kept on the long road of obedience.

Until they came to Haran.

There, for whatever reason, their journey stalled, and they settled down. How long did they stay? Long enough for Abraham to pile up some money and enlarge his staff of household servants (Genesis 12:5). But don't you detect a somewhat plaintive tone in the middle of chapter 11, verse 31?

> They went out with them from Ur of the Chaldeans to go to the land of Canaan; and they came to Haran and dwelt there.

Yes, it truly was a great start. But God is far more concerned with finishes. Sure, Haran was quite a ways down the road, but it wasn't far enough. The city lies near the five-hundred-mile mark of an eight-hundred-mile journey. Abraham's father, Terah, who had set out for Canaan with the rest of the family, got five-eighths of the way there. But he never did make it to Canaan; he died at Haran.

Scripture doesn't tell us why they stopped...but we might speculate a little. Was old Terah fed up with the journey? Had he found something in Haran, a flourishing city on the caravan route, that attracted him? The moon-god was worshiped at both Ur and Haran, and since Terah was an idolater (see Joshua 24:2), he probably felt at home in either place. Quite possibly, Haran seemed a lot like home, back in good ol' Ur.

"Canaan?" Terah might have mused. "Well, that might as well be the moon. Who knows what waits for us there? But, now, take Haran. It's settled, solid, secure enough...comfortable."

Who knows? Terah might have bumped into some old cronies...guys feeding pigeons as they reclined on some park bench, reducing life's adventure to a stalemate. In any case (though we can't know for sure), it looks as though the family settled in Haran at Terah's request. We can safely deduce that from the Word, because as soon as Terah died, Abraham, Sarah, and Lot got back on track. They resumed their journey to Canaan.

Scripture doesn't draw any conclusions. I don't mean to suggest Terah went to hell because he didn't do the will of God. It just says that he never arrived at the place of God's highest destiny for him and his family. He started out on a journey that he never really finished. He was more than halfway to the Promised Land—to God's possibilities—but he pulled up short.

It can happen with any of us. We can find ourselves living out our days in Haran. At any point we can let our lives stall out in a gray twilight zone of hesitation and indecision. Neither in Ur nor in Canaan. Neither here nor there. Neither hot nor cold. Neither where we were nor where we ought to be.

Perhaps you started out with the Lord on a journey of faith. He said, "I'm calling you to make a change. I'm calling you to head in a new direction toward a new destination." You started to follow. You made the break. You left old ways and old associations behind. You actually got quite a ways down the road. But then you came to Haran, to a place of familiarity and comfort...and you stopped following. That's as far as you got.

Friend, you can *die* in Haran.

I'm not talking about an eternal separation from God. I'm just talking about never realizing the Lord's purpose in your life. One poet has spoken of people "who died as though they'd never lived." How sad! How sad it would be to stand before the Lord Jesus someday and realize how different life could have been if we had wholeheartedly pursued His will.

Abraham and Sarah must have found Haran comfortable too. They may have found themselves thinking, "Isn't this far enough? Isn't this good enough? Isn't this sacrifice enough? Don't we get credit for leaving Ur and making a good start?"

Deep in his heart, however, Abraham knew his journey wasn't finished. And not long after they had finished at Terah's freshly dug grave, I imagine him gathering his family and saying, "C'mon. It's time to move on. We've been here long enough." So for a second time the clan packed their belongings and launched forth again—off toward a place and a future that was an utter mystery to them. Once again they left the familiar and the comfortable behind to follow the voice of the Lord.

Friend, it is the easiest thing in the world to go only as far in the will of God as those around you want to go. To advance as far as they advance. To stop when they stop. To coast when they coast. To be satisfied when they are satisfied. Paul had a word for the kind of people who measure themselves by the standards of others. He wrote: "They are only comparing themselves with each other, and measuring themselves by themselves. What foolishness!" (2 Corinthians 10:12, NLT).

The Lord's call is to *you*. His will is for *you*. The people around you may or may not feel comfortable and easy about where He's calling you to go and what He's calling you to do. But it's the Lord to whom you must answer, and He is the One who not only knows the end from the beginning, He knows you better than you know yourself. If Abraham had listened to his friends, he would have never left Ur. Or he would have hung it up in Haran. And, most likely, you and I would at this moment be considering the life of someone else, instead of a patriarch once named Abram.

NO ONE SAID IT WOULD BE EASY!

> Then Abram took Sarai his wife and Lot his brother's son, and all their possessions that they had gathered, and the people whom they had acquired in Haran, and they departed to go to the land of Canaan. So they came to the land of Canaan. Abram passed through the land to the place of Shechem, as far as the terebinth tree of Moreh. And the Canaanites were then in the land. (Genesis 12:5–6)

On my numerous trips to the Holy Land, I've seen historic signs of what the phrase "the Canaanites were in the land" implies: archeological evidence of a tragically and destructively depraved culture. As God speaks with Abraham in Genesis 15:16, He says, "The sin of the Amorites"—the most corrupt of the tribes among the Canaanites—"has not yet reached its full measure" (NIV). His stern words are God's way of saying, "The time is coming when I will be forced to expel these people from this land because of their evil. But that day of judgment hasn't arrived yet. I am still mercifully offering them the opportunity to repent."

When we read of the Canaanite presence, the Bible is not stating that a certain people already inhabited certain real estate. Far more than that, we're shown how an unhealthy, unholy quality of life reigned in the region—a quality that nauseated God. What was going on in Canaan was a sickening stench in God's nostrils, not because He arbitrarily "didn't like" their cultural lifestyle, but because God hates sin! And He hates it because it destroys His beloved creature—man. Thus, the "outcry" against the cities on the plain reached to the very heavens (see Genesis 18:20–21).

Into the middle of that darkness and sin and chaos, God called His man. Abraham, walking in the Lord's will, found himself squarely in the center of a culture that was an abomination to God.

That's the way it has always been. That is God's intention for His redeemed children, that we might "become blameless and harmless, children of God without fault in the midst of a crooked and perverse generation, among whom you shine as lights in the world, holding fast the word of life" (Philippians 2:15–16).

Many of us view the will of God as some kind of daisy-lined, yellow brick road that leads us from one peak of ecstasy to another until we eventually land on heaven's doorstep. But following God's will is not that way. It wasn't that way for Peter or Paul or John or Stephen—or so many other dear saints of God down through the centuries. In fact, God's will can lead us directly into some dark places, heavy times, and difficult circumstances.

When I was in Megiddo some time ago, I saw an excavated altar of the Canaanite religion. It was a huge circular structure built of stones—perhaps the size of a small church auditorium. As we stared at that ancient structure, a cold shudder ran through me. I was struck by the realization that upon that very altar before us gallons upon gallons of blood had been spilled in countless human sacrifices. Murder, torture, and unspeakable sexual perversions were integral parts of Canaanite worship. It was a dark, violent, demonic religion.

And think of it! It was to *this* place that God called and led Abraham and his family.

Maybe you've heard people say, "How can you really pursue the will of God in a time like this? It's such a godless world. Our culture has become so violent and sex-crazy. There's so much filth, so much corruption, so much immorality, so little regard for God." And we find ourselves caught up and locked up by the deterioration of the dying world around us. We think, "What a horrible era to try to live for the Lord. What a terrible time to bring up children!"

Folks, everything's different, but nothing's changed.

And for that matter, everything's changed but nothing's different!

God is still calling people to stand for Him in the middle of dark days and godless circumstances. He says, "I want to use you and speak through you. I want the life of My Son to shine through your life. You will be a light in the darkness. A tang of salt in a tasteless culture. A city on a hill."

CALLED FROM OUR COMFORT ZONES

Now the LORD had said to Abram:
"Get out of your country,
From your family
And from your father's house,
To a land that I will show you."
(Genesis 12:1)

The "country" in this verse refers to the *familiar*.

"Get out of your country," the Lord told Abraham. Anyone who has so much as crossed the California border into Tijuana, Mexico, knows that the minute you "get out" of this country you're in a whole different dimension. How unfamiliar everything there seems! It's not just some kind of chauvinistic patriotism that causes a person to say, "God bless America, land that I love." This is a delightful country we live in; there's nothing like it anywhere in the world. It's wonderful to come home after being on foreign soil. When you visit other lands—and some more than others, certainly—you're sensitive to the fact that you're away from your country and in the domain of the unfamiliar. Sometimes the strangeness can swallow you up, leaving you frightened, lonely, and depressed.

The truth is, any major move or change in our lives can leave us disoriented and insecure. Oddly enough, however, it is in these very situations that you and I may encounter God as never before. These are the times to seek His face and His will with renewed intensity.

When God calls you to do His will, He may very well wrench you away from that which is familiar to you—that which causes you to build your security upon things you know, rather than upon what you know of Him.

I'm not saying the Lord is going to move you to a little weather station in Antarctica or a tree house in the Amazon jungle. I'm not saying He'll pluck you from the shores of California and plunk you down in New England—or *vice versa*—but I am saying the Lord will stretch you in the area where you find your security.

When you stop to think about it, everything that we hang onto for security in this world is only temporary. It's like clinging to a deck chair on the *Titanic* as it slowly slips beneath the waves. We have no permanent abiding place in this world. Everything of this earth will pass away.

Paul wrote: "For the form of this world is passing away" (1 Corinthians 7:31).

John said: "And the world is passing away, and the lust of it; but he who does the will of God abides forever" (1 John 2:17).

Peter, typically, was even more blunt about it: "The heavens will disappear with a roar; the elements will be destroyed by fire, and the earth and everything in it will be laid bare. Since everything will be destroyed in this way, what kind of people ought you to be?" (2 Peter 3:10–11, NIV).

Even now, the world is coming apart around us. I don't need to list the evidence supporting that statement—it's everywhere. Our former sources of security are letting us down.

People talk about the relative "safety" of stocks or bonds or real estate or annuities or precious metals. But the fact is, *everything* this world is built upon has a shaky foundation. Realizing this, there's more and more need for us to adopt the attitude of Abraham:

> By faith Abraham obeyed when he was called to go out to the place which he would receive as an inheritance. And he went out, not knowing where he was going. (Hebrews 11:8)

I love that. *He went out...not knowing where he was going.*

"Where ya goin', Abraham?"

"Don't know."

"Well...why are you doing it?"

"Because the Lord called me."

"But—that's incredible! Do you mean you're going to follow God and you don't even know where you're going?"

"Listen. When I follow God, I *know* where I'm going—I just don't know the coordinates."

It is a more certain proposition to follow the Lord, not knowing where you're going, than to *think* you know where you're going and you're not following the Lord! Abraham had little idea of what lay ahead of him. He knew he wouldn't end his days in a rocking chair in Ur or a nursing home in Haran...but what would happen? What would it be like? He didn't know, other than that God had told him, "I will bless you."

In the same way, Jesus said to the young men who would be His disciples, "Follow Me, and I will make you fishers of men" (Matthew 4:19). He didn't fill in many of the blanks. He didn't tell them much about the price of discipleship. And I believe there's a reason why the Lord rarely reveals details about such matters at the beginning of our faith journey. I honestly doubt many of us would think we were equipped to deal with what lies ahead. We would look at what's down the trail and say, "Whoa! I could never handle *that*." But the Lord is going to build sons and daughters—strong men and women—in His purpose. These will be people who, as they mature and develop, *can* handle the pressures and trials that come along. And they will be fruitful, according to His purpose and design for them.

So the Lord summons us, calls us out from where we are, and says, "Leave your securities and comfort zones behind, and I will show you what I can accomplish through your life."

While on a visit to the Middle East some years ago, a group of us on our tour held a worship service on the banks of the Nile River. It was Sunday night, and we'd had an extremely full day, enduring a rigorous schedule of sightseeing and study. Everyone was weary. Yet as we gathered that night, we sensed the Holy Spirit speaking to our hearts. The essence of His message to us was this: "I can teach you things in this place that I could never teach you in your hometown. You're in an unfamiliar place, a strange land. But I want you to realize that throughout your entire lifetime, you are *always* away from your home. Not just when you are in a foreign nation, as right now; not just when you are in an unfamiliar city; and not just when you are in a hotel room, so far from familiar surroundings. Because My people have no abiding place in this world, you are *always* away from home...so fix your eyes upon that city where you're going."

There's an old song we used to sing when I was a teenager attending Youth for Christ rallies. We always finished the rallies singing: "With eternity's values in view, with eternity's values in view, may I do each day's work for Jesus, with eternity's values in view." A few years later I learned another chorus: "I can almost see that city just beyond yon distant hill, the city of my abiding, as God my Father wills. So I'll press more steadily onward; soon I shall see my King. I can almost see that city; already I hear God's angels sing."

We need to keep eternity's values in view and our eyes on the heavenly city—that's the message of Hebrews 11, where it speaks with praise of Abraham, who took a step of faith and became, according to Romans 4, the father of all who are called people of faith.

The passage goes on to say, "These all died in faith, not having received the promises, but having seen them afar off were assured of them, embraced them and confessed that they were strangers and pilgrims on the earth. For those who say such things declare plainly that they seek a homeland.... But now they desire a better, that is, a heavenly country. Therefore God is not ashamed to be called their God, for He has prepared a city for them" (Hebrews 11:13–16).

Praise God! You may spend your life in a tent, but you're going to end up in a city!

GOD'S CALL FOR COMMITMENT IS MUTUAL

"Get out of your country...
To a land that I will show you.

I will make you a great nation;
I will bless you
And make your name great:
And you shall be a blessing."
(Genesis 12:1–2)

God said at least three things to Abraham here. "I will show you a land…I will make you a great nation…I will bless you and make your name great."

What an extraordinary commitment! And it speaks of something wonderful about our Lord. He never calls you and me to step out into the darkness on faith without saying, "And this is what *I'm* going to do." In return for Abraham's obedience, the Lord promises blessings beyond that which Abraham has ever known.

The Lord will always call you to build your commitment to Him on commitments He has already made to you in His Word. He has promised to be with us always, to guide our steps, to hear our prayers, to bless the work of our hands, to give us His wisdom, His love, and His peace. And with those assurances in our hearts, He expects us to step forward in obedience and walk in His will.

God didn't ask Abraham to leave for an unknown land without first giving him a promise and a commitment. But keep this in mind: When the Lord makes a commitment *to* you, He also calls for a commitment *from* you. God said to Abraham, "You make that journey of faith, and I will make a nation out of you. I will make your name great."

And with that, Abraham went to his bedroom and started packing.

YOUR OBEDIENCE TO GOD'S WILL AFFECTS MORE THAN YOU!

The frightening thing about the summons of God on our lives is that it is never an isolated, independent transaction. Your response—or lack of response—always impacts others. We do not live this Christian life unto ourselves! Look at Genesis 12:5:

> Then Abram took Sarai his wife and Lot his brother's son, and all their possessions that they had gathered, and the people whom they had acquired in Haran, and they departed to go to the land of Canaan. So they came to the land of Canaan.

The Bible specifically mentions that when Abraham finally arrived, Sarah was with him, Lot was with him, and a whole tribe of others were with him. That sounds fine on the surface, but the more I think about that passage, the more it concerns me. My friend, the alarming thing about your and my response to the call and summons of God on our lives is that if we don't go, if we fail to obey, if we resist God's call, it's very likely there are other people who aren't going to be in the will of God either.

Something in us resists that notion, doesn't it? But consider with me...what if Abraham had never answered God's summons and had stayed in Ur? Or what if Abraham had stalled out in Haran and never finished the journey to Canaan? Would Sarah and Lot and the others have made it to the Promised Land? Would they have escaped the idolatry of their extended families? Would they have ever known the rich blessing of the Lord God?

We can't say for sure, but it doesn't seem likely, does it? That thought may make us uncomfortable. We might say, "I don't like to think that. Isn't finding the will of God for their lives *their* responsibility?"

Yes and no.

Yes, each person must respond individually to the Lord; and yes, God is well able to lead individuals along the path of obedience and blessing even when those in authority over them resist His will. But the Bible also notes that the Lord places people in positions of great responsibility, influence, and accountability over other lives, and Abraham was in such a position. Abraham was the covering for many people. Lot, his brother's son, was now as his own son. Sarah was his wife. The servants were also their dependents. And if Abraham didn't obey the Holy Spirit, what chance did *they* have of entering into God's abundance and blessing in Canaan?

Each one of us has a circle of influence, whether we realize it or not. But I think this is a message particularly to those of us who are the heads of homes. If Abraham had been content to stay in Haran, Lot and Sarah and all the rest of the family would have died in Haran, just as Terah did. Abraham accepted the responsibility for his entire family, and all of those attending them, and set out for Canaan.

You and I may think that if we fail to follow the Lord and provide spiritual leadership for our families that we are only affecting ourselves. *Be very careful about that attitude!* Jesus gave the sternest possible warnings to those who live in such a way as to cause little ones to stumble.

Whether we like it or not, or wish it were so or not, our lives have an impact. Others who are depending upon us may miss even the will of God if we deliberately ignore it.

IF YOU DO THE WILL OF GOD, HE WILL MANIFEST HIMSELF TO YOU

> Abram passed through the land to the place of Shechem, as far as the terebinth tree of Moreh. And the Canaanites were then in the land. Then the LORD appeared to Abram. (Genesis 12:6–7)

Hallelujah! The most glorious thing about doing the will of God is that as you do, the Lord will reveal Himself to you. It may be in dramatic, unforgettable ways. It may be in quiet, deeply reassuring ways. But that special manifestation of His presence is for those who obey Him.

In John 14:21, the Lord Jesus says, "He who has My commandments and keeps them, it is he who loves Me. And he who loves Me will be loved by My

Father, and I will love him and manifest Myself to him."

What does *manifest* mean? In the original language, the term means "to appear, to come to view, reveal, make visible, present oneself to the sight of another, to be conspicuous."

To whom does He reveal Himself in such a way? To those who have heard His call and allow themselves to be wrenched away from the earthly pattern of things, moving ahead in God's will.

These are the people who see God at work in their lives.

These are the people who experience His power.

Though we live in a culture that has drifted far from Him and even denies His name, He has placed a path before us. And His Word tells us: "Whether you turn to the right or to the left, your ears will hear a voice behind you, saying, 'This is the way; walk in it'" (Isaiah 30:21, NIV).

To *follow on* is to continually be *led* on—*to God's fullest and best*. There is no need to wonder, "If I *start* on the path of God's will, can I be sure I can *stay* on it?" Why? Because at each stage of His unfolding purpose, He will manifest Himself afresh. We've all seen a rocket shot exhaust the energy of its first stage just to break free of earth's confinement. Then a second stage kicks in, and the missile surges upward. In the same way, God's multiple and mighty resources in the Spirit are promised to attend us at each stage of His unfolding will for our lives.

He will manifest Himself, not only to lift us to the *skies*, but to thrust us even higher—to the *stars*.

[1] For ease of reading, I have chosen to use the names Abraham and Sarah throughout the chronology of their story, even though they were earlier known as Abram and Sarai.

CHAPTER TWO

Muddling Your Way in the Will of God

Abram passed through the land to the place of Shechem, as far as the terebinth tree of Moreh. And the Canaanites were then in the land. Then the LORD appeared to Abram and said, "To your descendants I will give this land." And there he built an altar to the LORD, who had appeared to him. And he moved from there to the mountain east of Bethel, and he pitched his tent with Bethel on the west and Ai on the east; there he built an altar to the LORD and called on the name of the LORD. So Abram journeyed, going on still toward the South.

Now there was a famine in the land, and Abram went down to Egypt to dwell there, for the famine was severe in the land. And it came to pass, when he was close to entering Egypt, that he said to Sarai his wife, "Indeed I know that you are a woman of beautiful countenance. Therefore it will happen, when the Egyptians see you, that they will say, 'This is his wife'; and they will kill me, but they will let you live. Please say you are my sister, that it may be well with me for your sake, and that I may live because of you."

So it was, when Abram came into Egypt, that the Egyptians saw the woman, that she was very beautiful. The princes of Pharaoh also saw her and commended her to Pharaoh. And the woman was taken

> to Pharaoh's house. He treated Abram well for her sake. He had sheep, oxen, male donkeys, male and female servants, female donkeys, and camels. But the LORD plagued Pharaoh and his house with great plagues because of Sarai, Abram's wife. And Pharaoh called Abram and said, "What is this you have done to me? Why did you not tell me that she was your wife? Why did you say, 'She is my sister'? I might have taken her as my wife. Now therefore, here is your wife; take her and go your way." So Pharaoh commanded his men concerning him; and they sent him away, with his wife and all that he had. (Genesis 12:6–20)

BLUNDERING INTO A MUDDLE

See if you can identify with this experience.

The Lord begins to show you something of His will and purpose for your life. Your days begin to take on new purpose and direction. Puzzle pieces that never seemed to fit together before suddenly fall into place, forming a picture that excites you. You feel (at last!) as though you've stepped up to a new phase in your Christian life—and you don't want it any other way.

Then, without warning, you find yourself stumbling headlong into circumstances so confusing, so troublesome, that you begin to wonder if you were on track with God in the first place!

Don't feel alone if you know exactly what I'm talking about. I imagine nearly every one of us who has hungered after the purpose of the Lord in his or her life has experienced something similar at one time or another.

Most likely you waded into that messy situation because you were still young in learning the will and way of the Lord. You may even now be young in the Lord...but that doesn't mean you have to undergo the sort of experience Abraham fell into. The Bible says we can benefit, vicariously, from the experience of others. In fact, Abraham's misadventures in this chapter are recorded in Scripture for our benefit. Paul insists that this is so. He writes:

> For whatever things were written before were written for our learning, that we through the patience and comfort of the Scriptures might have hope. (Romans 15:4)

This great man, Abram who became Abraham, the one we rightly call "Father of the Faithful," a patriarch as claimed, honored, and revered as any in the Scriptures, blundered headlong into about as stupid a situation as you can imagine.

Some of us who have slid and slithered into circumstances just about as deep don't have to imagine. The experiences are all too vivid in our memories!

How do children of God get into this kind of quandary? And how do we find our way out? Let's consider these questions as we look closely at the trouble Abraham created for himself as he muddled forward, fumbling his way in pursuit of the will of God.

Genesis 12:1 says, "The LORD had said to Abram: 'Get out of your country... to a land that I will show you.'" In verse 7 we're told: "Then the LORD appeared to Abram and said, 'To your descendants I will give *this* land.'" Notice that the Lord said, "I will show you a land," and when Abraham got there, He said, in effect, "*This is it.* This is the land. You're here." There could have been no confusion about it.

Acknowledging the holy significance of that moment, Abraham built an altar there at Shechem. After that (for no clear reason) he moved a little farther down the road, built another altar at Bethel, and pitched his tent in that place for a while. It was here, we are told, that Abraham "called on the name of the LORD."

In chapter 13 of Genesis, we find that Abraham and his family eventually returned to that place, Bethel, where he had pitched his tent. He came back to the altar he had built and, once again, "called on the name of the LORD" (v. 4).

Both of those moments are certainly among the high points in Abraham's life journey. But sandwiched *in between* them is an episode that is anything but high, noble, or spiritual. Amid these two events, the Bible records a string of occurrences that seem to have nothing whatsoever to do with the will or the purpose of God in Abraham's life! We're going to see God at work preserving and protecting Abraham and his family during this "interlude," but there is no evidence Abraham even once heard God's voice during that time—or made a single move according to the Lord's leading.

WAITING ON THE LORD

Recently in my studies I came across a little notation I'd jotted down years ago on this chapter of Scripture. I wrote "The Case of the Antsy Saint."

Somehow the title fits. Abraham just couldn't seem to stand still in the will of God. He got restless—*antsy,* as they say. He got the proverbial "itchy feet" and kept moving on a line that began in the will of God and then extended beyond it. His movement created problems, problems that seem to begin with Genesis 12:9: "So Abram journeyed, going on still toward the South."

I think there's wisdom here for us—and it may explain what's wrong when the average believer finds himself confused, muddled, or perplexed by where he is. So often in our lives we tend to be "going on still," rather than *standing* still.

These words describe how Abraham left the place where God had appeared to him and confirmed his ownership of the land. How he left the place where he had raised altars to His name. How he left the place where he, with his family, had called on the name of the Lord. Rather than waiting on God for direction, Abraham kept on the move. He kept drifting south...until he had drifted right out of the land of promise!

When I think of that biblical phrase "going on still," I can't help but contrast it with Moses' command to the Israelites. The whole assembly, roughly two million people, had gathered anxiously on the shore of the Red Sea with the Egyptian army in hot pursuit. And in that moment of sheer terror, the authoritative voice of Moses rang out: *"Stand still, and see the salvation of the LORD"* (Exodus 14:13).

Of course, the lovely thing about that particular situation was that they didn't have anywhere else to go! It's rather easy to "stand still" when you have the Red Sea in front of you and Pharaoh's army nipping at your heels. That may have been the origin of the old expression: "Between the devil and the deep blue sea." Maybe you've been there too!

When Moses commanded, "Stand still and see the salvation of the Lord," he was saying in essence, "Quit dancing around, quit fidgeting, quit whining, quit pulling your hair and biting your nails, quit trying to 'figure all this out.' Just stand still for a moment. Quiet yourself and watch the Lord go to work!"

The psalmist, one of the sons of Korah, had to come to the same place in his walk with the Lord. Perhaps he too had been "going on still" instead of "standing still" in the presence of God. But there came that time when he also heard the Lord's voice speaking to his heart:

> Be still, and know that I am God;
> I will be exalted among the nations,
> I will be exalted in the earth!
>
> (Psalm 46:10)

Many of us find ourselves "going on still" when if we would only *stand still* in our faith and *be still* in prayer and worship before Him, we would see God work in our lives as never before.

THE SIN OF PRESUMPTION

Most of us aren't quite so cornered as those Israelites, with their backs to the Red Sea. In most of our predicaments, we *can* identify options, find a back door, or cook up an escape plan. Yet even so, there is a great need to *daily* wait on the Lord. The Scriptures highlight this truth again and again.

One of the most graphic examples is in the Book of Joshua, concerning a little town with a little name: Ai.

At Ai, after the nation of Israel had conquered Jericho, Joshua said something to this effect: "Well, praise God, we got a victory there. Let's go take the *next* city." He had every reason to believe that since the Lord had blessed them in the battle of Jericho, the Israelites could continue to romp and stomp right through the rest of the land, conquering foes wherever they encountered them. After all, hadn't God said He was going to give them the land?

Consequently, they didn't bother to get down on their knees and seek out the Lord on the matter first. Joshua didn't bow before the "Commander of the army of the LORD" as he had before the battle of Jericho (Joshua 5:14). As a result, Israel's warriors were soundly defeated in battle. They came *crawling* back and said, "Lord, what did we do wrong?" And God could have easily said to them, "Just one small thing; you didn't ask *Me* what you should do." If they had consulted Him (the Commander!), they would have learned that one among their number was living in defiance to the Lord and His commands so that He could not bless them in battle as He had done at Jericho. The situation had changed, but they were still operating on an old set of battle plans.

This is a reminder to you and me.

We *never* move beyond our need for saying, "Lord, what will you have me to do *today?*"

We *never* move beyond our need to ask God for daily guidance.

We *never* move beyond our need to kneel before the Lord each morning and night and say, with David, "Search me, O God, and know my heart; try me, and know my anxieties; and see if there is any wicked way in me, and lead me in the way everlasting" (Psalm 139:23–24).

Years ago the Lord taught me one of the most precious lessons in the faith-life that I have ever learned. And it was simply this: Though I may become increasingly mature as a son in God's purpose, *I never will get past being a child in my need of Him!* We may become mature sons or daughters in the Lord but never forget: You and I will always be dependent children. No amount of growth or maturity will change that, even though our experience of years and deeper grasp of God's Word may tempt us to suppose we have passed beyond such need.

The finest saints succumb to this delusion at times—running ahead of the Father, relying on their own strength, wisdom, or personal experience. And it can lead the best of us straight into the sin of presumption.

Jean Firth was a great pioneer missionary who, with her husband, John, broke the ground that has resulted in one of the greatest ongoing harvests in the Americas. Before her homegoing to glory, I remember her sharing an experience with Anna and me...one that has lingered in my memory down through the years.

Jean was flying over the Andes Mountains in a World War II relic that should have been retired years before. That this antique of the forties was part of a South American airline fleet was not reassuring—especially considering the way it creaked and groaned its way above those craggy, towering peaks on that particular day.

Suddenly the ancient craft encountered turbulence, and the plane was shaking like a leaf, with every seam seemingly stretched. Jean wasn't just nervous, she was truly frightened for her life. As the plane kept shaking violently—suddenly dropping, then shooting upwards in a series of furious downdrafts and updrafts—she clutched the edge of her seat, pale and half-sick. In desperation she whispered in her heart, "Lord, I wish You would speak to this turbulence the way You spoke to the sea and ceased its tossing."

In that moment the Lord spoke quietly to her heart and said, "*You* speak to it."

She was a little taken aback by this but quietly intoned, "All right. In the name of Jesus I command this turbulence to cease!"

Instantly the turbulence stopped, and the plane flew along quietly—accompanied by an audible sigh of relief from the shaken passengers.

About twenty-five minutes later, however, the violent turbulence began again. So she repeated the words, "In the name of Jesus I command this turbulence to cease!"

This time, however, nothing happened. The turbulence didn't stop but continued—as frightening as ever. Jean went back to the Lord in prayer, saying, "Lord, earlier I spoke to the turbulence and it ceased. But this time I spoke and it didn't cease. Why?" To which the quiet whisper seemed to reply to her heart, "Because this time you didn't *ask* Me what you should do about it."

There's a message in that story about sustained, childlike dependence. In essence it teaches us, "Just because you've found a key doesn't make you Lord of the key ring!" The Lord can and will deliver us. But hear me, please: *He won't do it the same way every time.* He won't use the same methods in every circumstance. He won't employ the same tactics for every battle, and it is presumption to think He will. The continuing life lesson for us all can be found in the words of those who have repeatedly expressed our real need to learn and relearn our absolute dependence upon the Lord.

> Day by day...
> Day by day and with each passing moment,
> strength I need to meet my trials here.
>
> Hour by hour...
> I need Thee every hour, most gracious Lord.
> No tender voice like Thee can peace afford.
>
> Moment by moment...
> Moment by moment I'm kept by His love;
> Moment by moment I've life from above...
> Moment by moment...O Lord, I am Thine!

In situation after situation Paul called believers to "pray without ceasing" (1 Thessalonians 5:17). Likewise, David prayed, "Lord, keep my feet from presumptuous sins. Keep my lips from presumptuous words" (see Psalm 19:13–14).

This is the secret to living with Jesus as Lord of our lives. He has a right to expect daily obedience, the right to direct the way we "walk in the Spirit" so that we "shall not fulfill the lust of the flesh" (Galatians 5:16). Oh, yes! Make no mistake, dear one, the Lord *is* patient *and* loving *and* kind. Indeed, His lovingkindness is better than life, and His goodness extends to *all* generations. For He is a precious and loving Lord who, with great understanding, will receive us in spite of our failures, whose ear is always open to our cries when we come to Him in time of need—when we've failed and when we've been disobedient. Yes, He *is* that kind of a Lord.

But at the same time, He is also the Lord who says, "Take up your cross and follow Me." He also says, "If you love Me, keep My commandments." He is our Master who calls us to pursue His will and will teach us how through an increasingly obedient walk.

And there isn't room for presumption in that walk.

There is a never-ending urgency to keep our accounts short with Him, to maintain a humility and dependency that refuses to claim the proposition, "Been there, done that!" Let us fixate on this truth: Neither you nor I will ever outgrow our need for today's bread, today's guidance, today's instruction.

RESPONDING TO THE LEAN TIMES

Scripture tells us that "there was a famine in the land" (Genesis 12:10) and Abraham kept drifting south until he finally left the land of promise and entered Egypt.

Would he have continued to dwell up north on the plain of Moreh, between Bethel and Ai, had there been no famine? The Bible doesn't say. All we are told is that he headed south, toward the Negev, and that he found famine in the land.

Something in me wants to say, "Abraham, if there's famine, why don't you head back up *north,* where you met God and He told you, 'This is the place'?" I would rather be in the middle of a famine in the place God told me I should be, than go to a place with a multitude of comforts—but no assurance that I'm where He wants me to be.

In the early years of exploding growth at The Church On The Way, we were extremely crowded. We were having multiple services, hundreds of people were coming and going, parking was hard to find, and it simply wasn't very comfortable. We were trying to figure out how we might knock out a couple of walls and expand the auditorium for more seating.

I remember that a number of people kept asking our leadership, "Why are we going to extend the auditorium when we could just build a new building or move into a bigger facility someplace else? Why don't we change locations? Why don't we just move?"

Actually there was a very good reason not to move. For several months we had sought the Lord on the matter, and He *told* us not to move. That's all there was to it. Without the Lord's directive to move, the leadership of the church knew we had no business going anywhere. And as it turns out, staying in that location was very important for us as a body—for a number of significant reasons.

It was better—so very much better—to endure the discomfort of crowding and congestion and parking hassles than to run ahead of God with some grandiose scheme. And in His time, of course, He gave us the direction we needed to meet the challenges of our growing flock. His answers are the best answers...even when you have to wait for them.

That's one of the lessons in this incident in Abraham's life. Do what God tells you to do, and learn to wait patiently on Him. Move when He says move...but not until! You're better off staying in a place of limited resources—and even danger—when you're where the Lord has placed you, than you would be wandering off without the Lord's guidance to a so-called land of security and plenty.

MOVING AHEAD WITHOUT GOD

Down in Egypt, Abraham would find he could fill his belly, but he was also going to get a bellyful of trouble. He learned you can have a full table and a full stomach...but also have a double helping of heartache.

So Abraham arrived in Egypt, and he did a very stupid thing: He instructed Sarah to tell the Egyptians she was his sister. To protect his own skin, he made his wife extremely vulnerable.

This lie is a little easier to understand, I suppose, if you consider the culture of the times; there was a whole different attitude toward women then than now, to be sure. But something else is also true: While Abraham lived in such an era, he nevertheless was a man called of God—a man the Lord was going to use as a model of someone who was *not* like the world around him. God was calling Abraham to be the prototype of a people who would love others, regardless of gender. And Abraham was blowing it.

Abraham said to his wife, "Sarah, say you're my sister, and they'll do well by me." As a matter of fact, they *did* do well by him.

> The princes of Pharaoh also saw her and commended her to Pharaoh. And the woman was taken to Pharaoh's house. He treated Abram well for her sake. He had sheep, oxen, male donkeys, male and female servants, female donkeys, and camels. (12:15–16)

Abraham was raking it in. That little southern swing seemed to be paying dividends. But there was a problem: The Lord hadn't given Abraham this plan of provision; he'd come up with it himself.

He employed his strategy and it *seemed* to be working. But this was not the Lord's plan...and Sarah's virtue and honor were on the brink of being severely compromised. So the Lord began to work judgment on those around Abraham: "But the LORD plagued Pharaoh and his house with great plagues because of Sarai, Abram's wife" (Genesis 12:17).

We can see that a sort of paradox had developed, and to me it's a strong indication that Abraham was not in the will of God at this time. The Lord had said in verse 2 of this chapter, "I will...make your name great; and you shall be a blessing." What kind of blessing was he to the house of Pharaoh? When they were battling with those apparently life-threatening plagues, did they feel blessed by this man's presence among them? It was a "blessing" they would have gladly done without!

When we operate within the will of God, it's natural for blessings to overflow on others around us. But if you and I start muddling through life outside the will of God, that overflow of blessing dries up and only barrenness remains. Rather than blessing those around us, we become a dry well, with nothing to offer but disillusionment and disappointment.

Why is it necessary that you and I walk in the will of God? Just for our own delightful experience? No, certainly not for that alone. Just as Abraham's life was destined to "be a blessing" to others, so our lives, as we keep in step with the Spirit, will be an encouragement and a refreshment to others. Psalm 1 speaks of a man who delights in God's ways being "like a tree planted by the rivers of water, that brings forth its fruit in its season" (Psalm 1:3). In his letter to the Romans, Paul said, "I know that when I come to you, I will come in the full measure of the blessing of Christ" (Romans 15:29, NIV).

How did Paul know that? He knew it because he was pursuing the will of God with all his heart. And when we are walking in the Spirit, walking in His will, our presence will have an outflow and an overflow of the life of Jesus Christ.

Key to remaining in God's will is simply to wait where the Lord tells you to wait and not to move until the Lord tells you to move. As I noted earlier, we aren't told whether there was famine on the plain of Moreh, where Abraham had set up his tents before heading south. For the sake of argument, let's suppose there *was* famine and hardship there. Abraham might have learned a vital truth about God just that much earlier in his life: *He is the God who provides, no matter what the circumstances.*

As you read these words, you may be in a difficult place right now. Please listen carefully: *That's no proof that you're out of the will of God.* A better argument that you're out of the will of God might be that you are doing very well—but people around you are drying up and experiencing problems because there's nothing flowing from your life.

I don't know how many times I've heard people say, "I just thank God everything's going so smoothly! The Lord gave me a new job, I've already received a raise..." and so on. These seemingly good things don't necessarily prove a person is in the will of God.

In my imagination I can hear Abraham at a testimony meeting down there in Cairo: "Bless God! The Lord appeared to me up there on the plains of Moreh. I raised my hand to God and built an altar for worshiping Him up there, between Ai and Bethel. I just came down here because things weren't too good there where I was. I came here"—of course he skips over the part about Sarah and the little shenanigan he pulled—"and ever since I got here God's just been blessing me good. Man, I've got favor with the government and everything. Got a lot back on my income tax—more than I expected—and it just proves God's with me."

It doesn't prove anything at all! Abraham was out of God's will on this little side trip, and others paid a price.

You may say, "You know, Jack, it sure doesn't seem right to me that the Lord plagued Pharaoh's house because of Abraham's cowardice and lack of faith." No...it doesn't necessarily seem "right" to me either, but then, do we know all the ways of the Lord? Do we know enough about God and His creation to criticize His decisions? Shall the things that have been shaped—you and I—say to the One who shaped us, "Why have You done this thing?" or, "Why have You made me this way?" (see Romans 9:20). Let's face it and remember well: Neither you nor I have any right to dictate the terms of how the universe or the affairs of this planet are going to be run. We simply need to seek out and follow God's will. The rewards will be in certain, eventual, manifest fruitfulness.

Are you like a tree planted by the rivers of water? Are you bringing forth fruit in your life that sustains and heartens and attracts the weary and thirsty ones around you?

Sink your roots where He plants you, and draw on His life. The fruit will come, just as He promised.

THE ROAD BACK

When the Bible says the Lord plagued the household of Pharaoh for Abraham's sake, the result was that it got Abraham out of his muddle. In His grace, the Lord preserved His servant even in the middle of his folly.

Why should the Lord be so patient with us? Blessed be His name, loved one, He *is* patient. Notice that the Lord did not come thundering down on Abraham in anger and judgment, but He moved in on the situation in a way that drew His servant out of the mess he got himself into and put his feet back on the right path...*the path home!*

Did you notice where Abraham wound up?

> And he went on his journey from the South as far as Bethel, to the place where his tent had been at the beginning, between Bethel and Ai, to the place of the altar which he had made there at first. (Genesis 13:3–4)

He ended up right back where he was at the beginning, when the Lord had said, "This is the place."

I don't know where you may be in your life right now. You may be just beginning to discover that there's such a thing as living life in the will of God. You may have been living such a life for a long time—and, like me, still be ready to admit you have more to learn. Or you may be facing very difficult, possibly heartbreaking circumstances.

Sometimes we simply can't discern or understand why the Lord allows certain things to happen. You may be facing difficulty because it's a test—something designed to profit you and to build your faith. Or your trouble may be from the hand of Satan, your enemy, who would love to wring the joy out of your life. Or your stressed situation may be the bitter fruit of your own muddling. But whatever our circumstances, *we won't find the answer we seek by running here and there and trying this, that, and the other. We will only find it by standing still and seeing the salvation of the Lord.*

Don't run to Egypt when you've got problems.

Don't cook up your own defensive schemes to face your fears.

Get on your knees before the Lord.

"Yes," you may say, "but what if it's the Lord's will for me to run to Egypt?" Listen, if you're on your knees before the Lord and He wants you in Egypt, He'll put wheels on those knees and move you there! When you wait on the Lord, He'll see that you get where He wants you to be. One of the most beautiful truths about the Lord's way with us is this: As long as we are fully committed to His will and purpose for our lives, He will *never* permit us to remain in confusion.

The first few words of chapter 13 tell us: "Then Abram went up from Egypt." That sentence has even more weight when we note how often Egypt is used in the Bible as a symbol of sin and the world spirit.

> Then Abram went up from Egypt, he and his wife and all that he had, and Lot with him, to the South [or, the Negev]. Abram was very rich in livestock, in silver, and in gold. (vv. 1–2)

There is a divinely gracious paradox in this story's ending. Abraham got to keep the wealth he acquired in Egypt and brought it out with him.

Can you believe it?

He fumbled, stumbled, and fell—and got up again, smelling like a rose! Oh, my! What a gloriously merciful Lord we have! Even in our foolishness, even in our defeats, even in our blindness and disobedience, He showers His love and grace. And this is particularly true when our muddling disobedience is the result of sheeplike ignorance. Calculated rebellion and willful disobedience is one thing, but apparently in God's eyes the muddling child can find mercy.

Did Abraham know better? Was he in a rebellious frame of mind? Frankly, I don't see that in Scripture. What I do see is a man who could have saved himself a great deal of embarrassment and grief and wasted time if he had listened more carefully and waited more attentively on the Lord. But he didn't, just as so very often you and I don't either. Even so, the Lord graciously led him out of Egypt and back to the Promised Land.

Praise God, there's hope for us all!

If we set our paths to pursue God's will, even amid our muddling failures, the Lord can somehow bring about a net gain of profit, perception, and understanding. In the case of so many of the foolish, ill-advised, blindly or hastily pursued things I've done in my own life, not only did God bring me out of the pit of sorrow and despair, He brought me through with something in my hand that made me stronger and wiser than I was before I stumbled.

Only an almighty God, a living Redeemer, can do that.

CHAPTER THREE

Settling Problems in the Will of God

Lot also, who went with Abram, had flocks and herds and tents. Now the land was not able to support them, that they might dwell together, for their possessions were so great that they could not dwell together. And there was strife between the herdsmen of Abram's livestock and the herdsmen of Lot's livestock. The Canaanites and the Perizzites then dwelt in the land.

So Abram said to Lot, "Please let there be no strife between you and me, and between my herdsmen and your herdsmen; for we are brethren. Is not the whole land before you? Please separate from me. If you take the left, then I will go to the right; or, if you go to the right, then I will go to the left."

And Lot lifted his eyes and saw all the plain of Jordan, that it was well watered everywhere (before the LORD destroyed Sodom and Gomorrah) like the garden of the LORD, like the land of Egypt as you go toward Zoar. Then Lot chose for himself all the plain of Jordan, and Lot journeyed east. And they separated from each other....

And the LORD said to Abram, after Lot had separated from him: "Lift your eyes now and look from the place where you are; northward, southward, eastward, and westward; for all the land which you see I give to you and your descendants forever. And I will make your descendants as the dust of the earth; so that if a man could number the dust of the earth, then your descendants also could be numbered. Arise, walk in the land through its length and its width, for I give it to you."

Then Abram moved his tent, and went and dwelt by the terebinth trees of Mamre, which are in Hebron, and built an altar there to the LORD. (Genesis 13:5–11, 14–18)

As we begin to walk in the will of God, one thing we all learn is that we don't walk alone. We find many other people journeying with us.

If we were walking alone, with no one else in sight on that pathway, I suppose it might be a peaceful stroll down through the years. There wouldn't be any disagreements or disputes. There wouldn't be hurt feelings or misunderstandings or ruffled feathers. But it would also be mighty lonely and uninteresting! As it happens, however, there are others who also seek God's will and walk beside us. And where there are people—even redeemed people—bound for the same destination, there is always potential for confusion or conflict. If there is never any threat of conflict where you live, work, or worship, then someone is probably too intimidated to speak up!

Upon their return to the land from Egypt, a conflict sprang up between the herdsmen of Abraham and his nephew, Lot. Apparently there was some pretty serious crowding between the two groups of servants and their growing herds of livestock. And just as it is today, tempers tend to boil over in hot weather and traffic jams.

One potential outcome of this conflict among herdsmen was that their strife might spill over onto Abraham and Lot themselves, putting *their* relationship at risk. In the Old West they had a name for that sort of flareup:

range war! It would usually end with an armed face-off between the two cattle barons, where one would say to the other, "This country ain't big enough for the two of us!"

But Abraham was God's man, and his growth in God's grace equipped him with a problem-solving capability from which we can all learn. The potential destructive showdown between the uncle and nephew never occurred. But we shouldn't let that pass as just another fact. There are principles to be gained here, and they merit our searching them out.

Abraham discovered what we must all admit at certain points in our lives: When you walk the way of the Lord with others following the same path, at times even the closest of our relationships will be tested. It's significant to recognize that Abraham, "Father of the Faithful" and one of the most noble men who has ever followed in the way of the Lord, realized his relationship with a close family member was in jeopardy.

It could happen to *any* of us.

The fact that we're walking in the will of God doesn't mean for a moment that we will be free of relationship struggles. On the contrary, we realize from Scripture that such conflicts are inevitable. And unless these disputes are resolved using biblical patterns, the body of Christ may suffer stumbling, division, and hurt.

GIVING: IT'S MORE THAN MONEY

If you've been a believer for very long, you've learned that to be a follower of the Savior is more than a worshipful, vertical relationship with your Creator. Beyond that beginning point, if the love of God is alive within my life through His Holy Spirit, it will manifest itself in my growing heart affection and concern for other members of the body of Jesus Christ. I'll be learning to love them dearly. John wrote:

> We know that we have passed from death to life, because we love the brethren. He who does not love his brother abides in death. Whoever hates his brother is a murderer, and you know that no murderer has eternal life abiding in him.
>
> By this we know love, because He laid down His life for us. And we also ought to lay down our lives for the brethren. But whoever has this world's goods, and sees his brother in need, and shuts up his heart from him, how does the love of God abide in him? My little children, let us not love in word or in tongue, but in deed and in truth. And by this we know that we are of the truth, and shall assure our hearts before Him. (1 John 3:14–19)

John tells us, *"And by this we know that we are of the truth."* How do we know this? Because we love not only in word but in deed also. That verse which talks about "shutting up the heart" ("bowels of compassion" in the old King James) makes it profoundly graphic—referring to a deep, "gut-level" relationship. It's *way down there* laying hold of us in the inner man. We're called to *care*—and to care *deeply*—about people. And further, if I close off that spirit of *giving of myself* and *my substance* to my brother or sister, I'm bluntly asked, "How can you say the love of God abides in you?" In truth, I really can't.

I used to read those words from John's letter and automatically assume he was speaking only about money. I thought that let me off the hook because as a young person, I barely had enough money to make it through the week. Later, when I got into the pastorate, I didn't even have that much! I thought I could argue my defense from this text; I didn't have "this world's goods," so how could I help "my brother in need"?

However, with great insistence and patience, the Lord has taught me through the years that *the giving of myself* is much more involved than my mere gifts of material resource. Of course, it certainly includes that. But the truth is, most people we deal with need understanding, affection, compassion, and patience far more than they need money!

People who are in need yearn for somebody to be concerned about them, for someone to offer a little time and understanding. (Never underestimate the healing power of a listening ear!) Most of the time, meeting another's need has relatively little to do with money. Often, writing a check is the *easy* way out, while giving of our time, our emotional energy, and our empathy requires a real sacrifice of love. It is a sacrifice that compels us to lean even more heavily on the Lord's strength and wisdom to make us sufficient to manifest *His* love in *His* way.

THE GIFT OF TIME

As the days and years go by, I'm more and more aware of the urgency for strong members of the body to make themselves available—*voluntarily*—for personal ministry to others.

In these days of transition into the twenty-first century, I believe people feel increasingly isolated and alone. In spite of cell phones, personal pagers, e-mail, voice mail, on-line "chat rooms," and all those other high-tech communication tools, there is crushing loneliness in our land. Children are lonely. Singles are lonely. Young couples are hungry for friends. Retired and elderly folks feel devalued and forgotten.

It ought not to be so in the body of Christ.

Some people, especially newer Christians, often need someone to care, to take them up in their arms—in a spiritual sense—and just hold them and maybe rock them awhile, as it were.

That's exactly what most of us do with our own young children. When they cry during the night, we respond to their need by holding them and rocking them back to sleep. The truth is, you may "hold" and "rock" some people for *years* before they finally grow up, learn how to wipe their own nose, and take care of their own spiritual life. And that's all right. There's a need for people who have time to do that. There's a need for people to offer themselves as the very comforting voice, the reassuring hands, the supporting arms, and the strong shoulders of Jesus Christ.

In a long list of "one another" scriptures in the writings of Paul, there is one we sometimes overlook. When the apostle was writing to the Corinthians about considerate, loving behavior in their communion dinners, he instructed them to "wait for each other" (1 Corinthians 11:33, NIV). The King James uses the old English phrase "*tarry* one for another."

I like that, the classic wording...*tarry one for another.*

Don't assume that your time is your own...*tarry one for another.*

Don't pretend that your Daytimer is the Bible...*tarry one for another.*

Don't just charge ahead on your own schedule, satisfying your own needs, caring only for your own concerns...*tarry one for another.*

Have time for each other. Why? Because we *belong* to one another, and we belong to the same Lord. Can you remember the feeling you had as a child when a group of adults or older children you were with began walking or running so fast you couldn't keep up? They didn't even notice they were outpacing you. Remember falling farther and farther behind and shouting, "Hey, wait up! Wait for me!"?

No one wants to be left behind. And mature believers who are keeping pace with one another in the will of God need to look over their shoulders now and then to see who might be lagging behind...and about to give up.

We may be on a tight, heavy schedule. We may want to be the first one out the church doors to the parking lot. But we really can't talk of pursuing God's will by ourselves because there are people all around us who are walking the same path—and some of them need our time...our wisdom...our perspective...our encouragement. In Philippians, Paul wrote: "Let nothing be done through selfish ambition or conceit, but in lowliness of mind let each esteem others better than himself. Let each of you look out not only for his own interests, but also for the interests of others" (2:3–4).

This doesn't mean we throw our own agenda or objectives aside. There was no man more mission driven and goal oriented than the Lord Jesus Christ when He was on the way to the Cross. In fact, writing prophetically, Isaiah captured the words and mind-set of the Messiah as He turned toward Jerusalem for the final time: "I have set My face like a flint" (Isaiah 50:7).

Nothing could deter Him from His objective. Nothing could turn Him from His task. He had His Father's will to fulfill, and there was a world that desperately needed a Savior. Yet think of this! On that final leg of His march toward the Cross, Jesus stopped along the roadside in Jericho to take time for a lonely, forlorn blind man who had raised his voice for mercy (Luke 18:35–43). The words etch themselves into our minds: *"Jesus stood still"* (18:40).

He stood still to take the time for blind Bartimaeus. He stopped in His tracks to respond to one man's voice. He stood still—and forever defined what it means to have compassion for people's needs. At the sound of this cry of the heart, Jesus turned aside, pushed through the crowds, touched a man, and healed him. What an example!

It is written! No matter what important or compelling demands claim my schedule, I—you and I—need to take time for one another.

Exactly as Jesus takes time for us.

PROBLEMS IN THE MIDST OF BLESSINGS

> Now the land was not able to support them, that they might dwell together, for their possessions were so great that they could not dwell together. (Genesis 13:6)

Jealous over their turf, the herdsmen started bickering with one another. I know the tensions crowding can bring about among people. We've had serious crowding problems at The Church On The Way over the years, and (I must admit) it's better than the opposite problem! But dealing with the push, the inconvenience, the complaints, and the tempers that a crowd can produce will test even the spirit of saints.

Abraham and Lot also had experienced prosperity and blessing—things were abounding around them. Yet all was not well: "There was strife between the herdsmen" (13:7).

Even in the midst of great blessing, you will find difficulties and problems. People-to-people problems. Snags in the relationships between men and women who are moving in the will of God and experiencing kingdom life together. People aren't perfect, and never will be, this side of heaven.

When the clash came between the herdsmen, Abraham went to Lot and said, "Let there be no strife." The principle here is this: *If you become aware of a point of strife, if a problem develops between you and a brother or a sister, then move directly to reduce it to zero. Seek to gently stop it instead of multiplying it and letting it escalate.* Taking care of the problem immediately as Abraham did is best, no matter what anyone may tell you. "Oh, let it go. It'll work out," sounds easiest, but silence, time, and separation are not the friends of reconciliation.

Don't let emotions harden and calcify. Don't let disputes deepen and fester. And...

> "Don't sin by letting anger gain control over you." Don't let the sun go down with you still angry, for anger gives a mighty foothold to the Devil. (Ephesians 4:26–27, NLT)

TO SOLVE CONFLICT, START WITH YOURSELF

> "Please let there be no strife between you and me, and between my herdsmen and your herdsmen." (Genesis 13:8)

The argument that started it all really didn't have much to do with Abraham and Lot. Most likely they weren't even in the vicinity when their servants began shouting insults and throwing elbows. Abraham, as Lot's uncle and head of the clan, was the authority figure in this situation. His word was the law of the land, and there was no other! But rather than barging noisily into the situation and dictating terms, the older man said in a gracious, gentle way: "Let there be no strife between you and me."

He didn't say, "Your herdsmen are getting to be a pain," or "Hey! Your guys are strong-arming mine. Bug off!" Rather, he took it immediately to the personal, relational level. "Let's not let anything come between you and me, Lot. Whatever it is, it really isn't worth it."

It's a beautiful principle for resolving people problems: *Start with yourself.* Don't immediately think in terms of how to fix the problem by "fixing" the other person. The lyrics of the old spiritual get at the truth of this principle: "It's me, it's me, it's me, O Lord, standing in the need of prayer."

Abraham didn't stop there, however. Listen to the most significant phrase in the text: "Let there be no strife...*for we are brethren.*" Hear it: *brotherhood.* Where he might have assumed his authority on the grounds of being Lot's uncle and guardian with years of maturity on him, Abraham chose to back off.

This dispute could have easily degenerated into something ugly. In my imagination I can hear all kinds of scenarios being played out. I can imagine Abraham walking around the tent, muttering, as Sarah prepares dinner. "You know, this is the third day in a row that Lum and Zum have come back and told me that Lot's herdsmen are hassling them over the south pasture. Who does Lot think he is? He wouldn't even *be* here if it weren't for me! Everything that kid knows he learned from me. Everything he owns is because of me. And *this* is the thanks I get?"

Abraham could have taken a tough approach with the younger man. "Hey, bud, listen up! You're the junior partner in this operation—you're my nephew and don't forget it. So back off!" Or imagine a snobbishly self-righteous, "I say unto thee, 'submit!'"

But it didn't happen that way. Instead, Abraham submitted *himself.* He said, "Beyond the strife, Lot, we're brothers. So take a long look at the land before us. I want you to be fruitful and fulfilled, so select which part of the land you would like. You choose. If you go right, then I'll go left, and if you go left, then I'll go right. Which way I go doesn't really matter. What matters is our relationship."

I believe Abraham did what he did and said what he said to Lot with a full, sincere heart. I don't believe there was any duplicity or guilt-mongering here at all. I don't think Abraham was saying between the lines, "Well, Lot, never let it enter your mind that God promised *me* the land. The *whole thing.* But (sigh), be that as it may...I want everything to be all right between us, so you just go ahead and take whatever you want. Far be it from *me* to let the voice of the Lord and the will of God get in the way of what *you* want." (All attended by violins, a heaven-cast, wearied gaze, and a light beating of the chest.)

I'm not just trying to be cute or clever here. Those divisive, manipulative words are exactly the kind spoken within the body of Jesus Christ every day. And, sadly, they are so very often credited with being in accord with the will of God.

When you think about it, God *did* promise Abraham that land! Yet the older man, without any grasping whatever, made a proposal—by a moment's decision—that could have caused him to lose what was rightfully his!

Here is a man who truly abandoned himself to the faithfulness of God: "Lord, I believe You gave me this land. But I am not going to let what I think is mine (at least as I understood Your voice) become a matter that divides me from my brother. Lord, I choose to leave it all with You."

Just a few chapters later, in another context, Abraham uttered the words: "Shall not the Judge of all the world do right?" And so it is here. He was content to leave his affairs in the hands of Heaven's Court. He knew that—ultimately—God's sovereign purpose would be realized, and he could rest in that.

Many of us would have said, "Well, my goodness, Abraham, you've got *every right* to contend for that land. You're *only in your rights* to hold that young man at arm's length and say, 'Lot, you move over there where I tell you.'" Yet what Abraham did was *trust the Lord*. He settled the dispute in the right way, and when it was over...he ended up still in the land.

Not only did he submit to Lot by saying, "Lot, you take first pick," but in doing so he was submitting to the Lord in simple trust and faith. Listen friend, there will be times in your relationships with other people when the only truly secure place you have to rest your case is with God. Yes, it's true...

> you may hold the moral high ground;
> you may be 100 percent right;
> you may be in accord with the will of God as you understand it;
> you may have your brother-in-law and three deacons who agree with you;
> you may have a dozen scriptures to buttress your case.

But instead of setting your jaw and contending for your "rights," it may be time simply to pray, "Lord, I rest my case with you," and then say, "My brother, my sister, you suggest a solution. I just want to have it right between us."

In the long run, the Lord will never let you suffer ill for such sacrifice. He's faithful to His promises. If He's a big enough God to make a promise, He's big enough to overcome obstacles in human relationships to fulfill it and keep it.

THE RISK THAT WASN'T

> Then Lot chose for himself all the plain of the Jordan, and Lot journeyed east. And they separated from each other. Abram dwelt in the land of Canaan, and Lot dwelt in the cities of the plain and pitched his tent even as far as Sodom....

> And the LORD said to Abram, after Lot had separated from him: "Lift up your eyes now and look from the place where you are—northward, southward, eastward, and westward—for all the land which you see I give to you and your descendants forever." (Genesis 13:11–12, 14–15)

Compare this passage with the simple promise God gave to Abraham in Genesis 12:7: "Then the LORD appeared to Abram and said, 'To your descendants I will give this land.'"

Abraham's vision had expanded since that first promise.

In the earlier encounter, the Lord had spoken to Abraham of a land. This time, the Lord gave him its *dimensions*. And it was as far as the man could see in any direction!

The will of God in your life and mine will always be a beautifully progressive revelation. There's a constant unfolding of His way, His will, and His purpose for our lives with the passing of seasons and years. God's new revelations never contradict what He has said before; the Lord is always consistent with Himself. But what we know of God's will is constantly expanding, developing, and flowering. And every now and then, our winding path of pursuing His will opens up to a vista that fairly takes our breath away!

Can you imagine the scene? Can you see the old man, standing on a high, windswept bluff in the long shadows of late afternoon, watching his nephew walk off toward the lush, green fields of the east?

What was going through his heart in that moment as the wind blew through his hair and flowing gray beard? Had he been foolish? Had he made the right decision? Had he given it all away? What would become of him and Sarah? And what of God's promise?

And then...there was that unmistakable voice—so powerful, yet so tender—speaking into the gathering twilight. *"Lift up your eyes now and look from the place where you are."*

Just look, Abraham. Let it fill your eyes. Let it overflow your heart and your memory and your dreams. Let the vision capture your heart. And Abraham looked. North. South. East. West. God told him, "All the land which you see I give to you and your descendants forever. And I will make your descendants as the dust of the earth; so that if a man could number the dust of the earth, then your descendants also could be numbered" (Genesis 13: 15–16).

God was saying, "Abraham, I'm going to people this land with your progeny, your offspring. People will come to life because of what I'm going to do in you."

Hear it, loved one: When we learn how to relate to people *in* His grace, then the Lord lets us become *begetters* of life *by* His grace. He makes spiritual fathers and mothers of such people. He enlarges our responsibilities. He expands our borders. Perhaps this provides insight into the reason some believers never really experience fruitfulness, seeing people brought to Jesus through their efforts. If people were to come to Jesus through the touch of some of us and were around us very long, they would be driven away again by our lack of gentleness and understanding. So the Lord uses other people to reach the unbelievers in our midst, and we find ourselves wondering, "Why am I not more fruitful?" The Lord wants to teach us that *all fruit comes from an obedient, loving response to His desire to work THROUGH our lives* in relationship *TO* other lives. The fruit of the Spirit—*first*—is love.

POSSESSING THE PROMISES

Initially God had said, "I will show you a land" (see Genesis 12:1). Then He said, "I will give you this land" (see Genesis 12:7). But now He was saying, "Look as far as you can see in every direction. Those are the dimensions of the land I'm giving you" (see Genesis 13:14).

After Lot left, the Lord had spoken, "Arise, Abraham. Walk in the land through its length and width, for I give it to you." And within these words to our faith-father, God gives us yet another great principle in pursuing His will:

We are to TAKE POSSESSION of what God promises us. This principle is found time and time again throughout Scripture, and it is applied by first capturing a glimpse of your "lot," that is, your promised, God-given inheritance.

David wrote: "The boundary lines have fallen for me in pleasant places; surely I have a delightful inheritance" (Psalm 16:6, NIV). Whatever God has promised us calls forth our active understanding and partnership. He wants you to reach by faith and possess it. God's best won't just fall into your lap; but as with Abraham, we are to go and tread on it.

God spoke the same way to Joshua, "Wherever the sole of your foot shall tread, I've given you that land." The Lord told the people repeatedly, "Go and possess all the land." So the principle is well established in His Word: When God unfolds His will to us, then we are to walk *into* it and actively embrace it. It's one thing to learn new facts of the Lord's will in His Word but quite another to choose to walk in them. It's a mistake to substitute mere information about God's will for active participation.

Some will say, "I like it where I am; it's comfortable here. And I've been blessed here." That may be so, but remember how Abraham was led by the Lord from one altar to the next. There were altars at Shechem, Bethel, and Hebron. Ask yourself, did building an altar in Hebron demean or diminish the one at Bethel? Not at all! It simply represented a further unfolding of God's will for Abraham's life. The Lord was leading him to an area of expanded revelation, expanded dimension in the purpose of God. And there at the new altar he raised testimony to the promises of God, and he offered sacrifice, an indication of pouring out himself in dependence upon God.

I believe with all my heart that some of us have been shown by the Lord a broader dimension of life; He is saying, "Now move on! Step out." He summons some, and yet they haven't gone to the new place—to build an altar there. Abraham could have said, "But, Lord, it's cozy here. After all, the tents are staked down, and there's a real nice view through our tent flap. There are springs nearby, and there's plenty of room for the flocks, now that Lot's moved on. Everything's dandy right here."

But the Lord was saying, "I've got greater things for you, and I'm summoning you to move on with Me." And so it was that Abraham moved out to new dimensions—across the land and forward in the purposes of God.

Some time ago I talked with a man who told me, "When it comes right down to it, Pastor, I guess my real problem is that the Lord showed me a while back that I was to do a particular thing...and I just didn't do it."

He was right. That *was* this man's problem. When the Lord shows you a larger area of walking in His will, then *go* there. Move on. Life in the will of God is never stale or stalemated. There are always boundaries of possibility beckoning us. Step out into God's tomorrow!

SEEK UNITY WITH YOUR ADVERSARY

Before we leave this promise-rich passage, I want to review one more principle that Abraham's response to Lot brings into focus. I believe that God's high promise of new and broader dimensions in Abraham's life only came as a result of the patriarch's refusal to let interpersonal tensions make him small.

Abraham didn't allow his dispute with Lot to become an obstacle that would trip him up in pursuing the will of God. Remember what Jesus said about interpersonal struggles?

> "Therefore if you bring your gift to the altar, and there remember that your brother has something against you, leave your gift there before the altar, and go your way. First be reconciled to your brother, and then come and offer your gift." (Matthew 5:23–24)

What's really being said here? You're not standing at the altar recalling that you have something against your brother. No, you remember that *he's* got something against *you*. You might be tempted to say, "Well, if he's got something against me, that's *his* problem. That's his responsibility." Yet look where

Jesus lays the responsibility when there's discord: "If you bring your gift to the altar, and there remember that your brother has something against you, leave your gift there before the altar, and go your way." In other words, the Lord is saying, "Don't even think about getting wrapped up in worship at this point. Get things worked out with your brother first."

In the next verse He says, "Agree with your adversary quickly, while you are on the way with him" (v. 25). This "adversary" could even be a brother or sister in the Lord, someone who is actually walking with you in the will of God. I used to read that passage and say to myself, "But I thought Satan was my adversary." Yes, he is certainly my adversary and my foremost opponent, but even people in the body of Christ can be adversaries. And Jesus says, "Agree with your adversary quickly." If somebody is pitted against you in a situation, the Bible says you should immediately begin working to create harmony between you. That word *agree* here means "of a good mind." Come to a good unity of mind together.

Jesus said, "When you know that your brother has something against you, *go to him.*" Keep in mind that if your brother has something against you, he usually has some grounds for it, at least in his own mind. So often we respond, "There wasn't any *reason* for him to feel that way!" "There wasn't any justification for her to say what she did!" Listen, if we could walk where he walks, think how she thinks, live where they live for just five minutes, we might understand that, from another's point of view, there was more than ample reason for being hurt or embittered by what you or I said or did.

Now, I'm not saying that in every case the other person is completely accurate in his or her assessment of things. But neither is it correct for us to stand aside and say, "Well, it wasn't right for her to feel that way! If she had any spiritual maturity at all..." We don't have the right to make such a judgment! Abraham, too, could have reacted that way: "Lot's just a nephew, anyway. He's acting like his daddy, ol' Haran, used to act when we were kids! Why doesn't he just grow up?"

Instead, he said, "I'll take the initiative. I'll make the first move. I'll take the loss, if there is to be a loss. After all...we're brethren."

Someday as we stand before the Lord, I believe we will be amazed to learn that even when we were "100 percent right" according to Scripture and according to everybody and everything that we knew, we really were *dead wrong* because of the attitude of our heart and our unwillingness to humble ourselves and reconcile. This is true even if we can accurately list every reason why the other party is at fault!

People often hurt us unintentionally. They have no particular ax to grind with us, no desire to harm us. Suppose Joe has wounded you—perhaps deeply. If you knew Joe's background, his past hurts, the heartaches he's endured, what has been eaten out of him by other people or past circumstances—if you knew *why* Joe responds to people and things the way he does—you would probably fall at his feet and weep for him. You'd pray for him, and love him, and walk with him! You would discover that people like Joe do not deserve your antagonism when they treat you without grace; they need compassion, love, and understanding so they can be healed.

The Lord sees people that way, not as we tend to view them. He looks on the heart...with a heart full of love.

FROM BITTERNESS TO BONDAGE

In the same passage dealing with relationships in Matthew 5, Jesus went on to warn: "Agree with your adversary quickly...lest your adversary deliver you to the judge, the judge hand you over to the officer, and you be thrown into prison. Assuredly, I say to you, you will by no means get out of there till you have paid the last penny" (Matthew 5:25–26).

In other words, you'll be imprisoned and you won't be released until the full price has been paid. I believe this scripture deals precisely with spiritual bondage resulting from bitterness and unforgiveness. What happens if you don't agree with your adversary? What happens if you cling to unforgiveness and the bitterness festers and festers? You'll find yourself in prison, and the release from that confinement will be neither easy nor cheap.

David once said, "Praise be to the LORD my Rock, who trains my hands for war, my fingers for battle" (Psalm 144:1, NIV). Did you know there are arthritic fingers in the body of Christ, due to unforgiveness? There are people who are twisted and bent and stiff because they pit themselves against a brother or a sister while the Lord wants to use them as a finger in the body of Christ—to draw back the bowstring and to set aim, sending a righteous arrow crashing into the forces of the enemy. He wants to use us to level some of the great foes of the kingdom of God, to burst in the walls of the powers of darkness. But there are crippled, ineffectual limbs, hands, and fingers in the body because of the stiffness and infirmity caused by our unwillingness to reconcile with others and forgive them from the heart.

It's a spiritual disease. It's spiritual bondage. It's spiritual prison. The scripture says you don't get out of this "prison" until you've *paid the price*. Yes, the price has already been paid for our eternal salvation, so we're not speaking of buying our way out of hell. But we can still spend our days here on earth locked up tight in the prison of bitterness and unforgiveness. The cost of release from that prison is a deep humbling of ourselves before the Lord and before those who have wronged us.

A willingness to bear the pain.

A willingness to forgive.

A willingness to pay the full price to redeem a relationship.

Jesus knows all about it.

PREPARATION FOR BATTLES AHEAD

Abraham went to Lot in humility of heart and said, in effect, "I feel things haven't been right between us. What can I do to help? We're brothers. Let's make our relationship good and strong again." In doing this—and without even knowing it—*Abraham was spiritually equipping himself for what lay ahead in his relationship with Lot.* Abraham's conflict-solving skills would be needed again—and soon—but in a much deeper crisis for much greater stakes. The issues were about to intensify dramatically.

In the very next chapter we will see what happened when Lot was captured in battle. Abraham would become God's instrument for rescuing a brother who had been taken at sword point and carried away. But listen...he would never have been qualified for that task if he hadn't first learned how to deal with personal squabbles and petty conflicts!

Once Abraham demonstrated his heart in the matter of the land dispute, he was prepared for an even greater battle. And it grew from there! Even later, when we come to Genesis 19, the Lord summoned Abraham to pray, to intercede on Lot's behalf. And he prayed for the city of Sodom, asking the Lord to spare that wicked place—for Lot's sake and the sake of any other followers of God who dwelt therein. And through the agency of Abraham's prayer *Lot would be lifted up and carried bodily out of the city.* It would happen because his brother in the Lord interceded for him.

The example of Abraham's relationship with Lot shines with magnificence in Scripture:

He is the instrument of understanding and grace in the land squabble.

He is the instrument of rescue when Lot is captured in battle.

He is the instrument of salvation when, by his prayers and intercession, he secures Lot's deliverance from the very pit of hell.

Reach out and pull your brother or sister to safety, even as "a burning stick snatched from the fire" (Zechariah 3:2, NIV). Love your brothers and sisters in the Lord; show them patience, kindness, and grace. When necessary, be the willing instrument of their rescue.

People savers.

That's what we are to become under the touch of the Lord, as we pursue His will in a world filled with irascible, unpredictable, cantankerous, needy people...people a lot like you and me.

CHAPTER FOUR

Warfare in the Will of God

> And it came to pass in the days of Amraphel king of Shinar, Arioch king of Ellasar, Chedorlaomer king of Elam, and Tidal king of nations, that they made war with Bera king of Sodom, Birsha king of Gomorrah, Shinab king of Admah, Shemeber king of Zeboiim, and the king of Bela (that is, Zoar). All these joined together in the valley of Siddim (that is, the Salt Sea). Twelve years they served Chedorlaomer, and in the thirteenth year they rebelled. (Genesis 14:1–4)

Strange sounding names in strange sounding places...dark times in a dark era of earth's early history. International conflict was brewing, with Canaan as its epicenter. Turbulent clouds of war banked the horizons, and tensions ran high.

Abraham and his family lived right in the middle of it, in the land to which God had called them. Would the warfare touch his family, too, or would it flow around them, like an island in a muddy river at flood tide?

The Bible tells us that it did indeed touch his family. Abraham would be involved in warfare up to his ears, whether he wanted to be or not.

And so it is with you and me, in the great spiritual warfare that swirls and rages all around us. The Bible clearly states that we, too, are at the center of conflict on a vast scale while we live out our days on this planet. This was true when the Bible was written, and it is unquestionably true today as well. Warfare sweeps around us everywhere. This Bible text describes physical warfare, but that only symbolizes the infinitely larger conflict that has gripped our world since the beginning of time—the spiritual contest we often sense but never see. It is the struggle that never relents...even when we are living in the middle of God's will and seeking to pursue it faithfully.

The apostle Paul describes that warfare in dramatic words:

> For we are not fighting against people made of flesh and blood, but against persons without bodies—the evil rulers of the unseen world, those mighty satanic beings and great evil princes of darkness who rule this world; and against huge numbers of wicked spirits in the spirit world. (Ephesians 6:12, TLB)

Consider what we see transpiring in the physical dimension of mankind:

—bodies destroyed by bullets and bombs
—homes split open by marital warfare
—relationships ripped apart at the interpersonal level
—gang warfare snuffing out young lives and spreading like a dark cloud across our urban areas
—babies slain by the millions in a hellish attack against the very sanctity of a mother's womb

All this turmoil and violence in the physical realm is a result of violent strife in the spiritual dimension. The spiritual war smolders and flames all around us, a bitter battle to the end, and you and I as believers are involved in it up to our ears...whether we like it or not.

We may at times feel awash in the tides of this vast spiritual battle...nothing more than helpless pawns unwittingly embroiled in a mighty cosmic clash of invisible superpowers. Some people of limited vision see us standing on the fifty-yard line of a football field—two great teams rushing upon us as we stand there quivering, wondering which one will hit us first or whether we'll be mashed between them like ham in a sandwich!

But no, we are not casual observers of this mighty conflict. We are not helpless beings at the mercy of evil powers with no role to play in the war's outcome. The Lord wants us to understand our true role in the present conflict.

THE POWERS OF DARKNESS IN TURMOIL

Four nations war against five across the text of Genesis 14. There was nothing picturesque or romantic going on here; this was not a case of good guys versus bad guys, the forces of righteousness battling the forces of unrighteousness. *None* of these groups carried the banner of righteousness. What is described is an ancient snapshot of the horrible strife still taking place in our world, fomented by the powers of darkness who war even among themselves.

One thing that may encourage you in this matter of spiritual warfare is the fact that in the Adversary's dark kingdom, there is no unity, only authority.

Here's what I mean. The structures of spiritual authority and the sheer brute power resident in demonic beings—the powers given them by God when they were first created and unfallen—have never been rescinded. Even after the rebellion that saw these now-become-dark beings expelled from heaven, God did not take back what He had given. He never does (Romans 11:29). Those powers are still present with those fallen creatures, despite their rebellion.

But there is a loophole.

Though their hatred is uniformly vented toward God and His own, they are not unified themselves. Never—even in their circle of hate—is there peace or unity. And certainly no friendship.

Incidentally, one of the most foolish things you will ever hear people say is, "Well, if I'm going to hell, at least all my friends will be there too. We'll just go right on partying!"

It may seem a clever quip. It might even get a laugh or two. But nothing could be further from the truth. The very thing that eventually divides all of us from physical life—our sin—also divides us from spiritual life until, or unless, we come back to life through Jesus Christ. That *separation,* that begins with physical death, only *intensifies* after death. The division so dramatically illustrated by the unbeliever's soul leaving his body is only the beginning of a process of *vast* division. Once separated from the hope of any relationship with the Lord of light, the downward spiral proceeds into an eternity of banishment into the darkness.

The Bible speaks of the horror of judgment, self-imposed through sin and unbelief. It describes the unbelievers' "gnashing of teeth," grinding in anguish against themselves *because no one else is there*. "The worm dies not," Jesus said, and "the fire is not quenched," describing an active conscience that exists forever in the awareness that "I *missed* it. I missed life! I missed heaven!" Hell is a lonely place where an individual is without home, help, or comfort forever.

You may say, "I don't like to think about such things. I'd rather read about the love of God." Listen, my friend: The love of God went to the utmost to deliver us from such a judgment.

> "For God so loved the world that He gave His only begotten Son, that whoever believes in Him should not perish but have everlasting life." (John 3:16)

The way to eternal light and eternal life is still wide open…for now. But when the door closes, it closes forever. So never mistake the blessing of God's good news: One whisper of Jesus' Name to heaven, and eternal hope and heaven's home are yours. "Whoever calls on the name of the LORD shall be saved," or delivered (Romans 10:13).

But here we are considering Abraham's warfare setting and being reminded of ours. As I said, there is no love lost among the cohorts of hell. Their cosmic lostness breeds an internal, intramural hatred among all beings confined to eternal judgment. The demons hate each other, not just God, you, and me. The psalmist asked, "Why do the nations rage?" They rage because they lie in the grip of dark powers, age-old enemies that hate and war against one another down through the generations and centuries. And that same Psalm 2 goes on to describe how they unite in their hatred of the Lord and His Anointed. But apart from that *banding*, there is no *bonding*—no unity among the powers of darkness.

That's good news for us! And it helps explain the raw power inherent in these words of Jesus:

> "Again I say to you that if two of you agree on earth concerning anything that they ask, it will be done for them by My Father in heaven. For where two or three are gathered together in My name, I am there in the midst of them.... And I will give you the keys of the kingdom of heaven, and whatever you bind on earth will be bound in heaven, and whatever you loose on earth will be loosed in heaven." (Matthew 18:19–20; 16:19)

That's part of the reason the Lord sent out His disciples in twos; they ministered in pairs of "agreement." This principle of pairing off against the powers of hell opens up exciting potential for ministry.

One day years ago Darrell, an associate pastor at the church, and I were out calling together. We were making contacts concerning an upcoming meeting at the church. In the process of making our routine stops, however, we found at least half a dozen individuals in deep need of help, encouragement, and counsel. In just a few short hours, we encountered sickness, burden, and concern.

Darrell and I hadn't anticipated anything like that. We'd simply decided to take a drive that day and make several stops, but the outing had become a powerful ministry opportunity—at almost every turn! As we were driving along to yet another appointment, I remember thinking to myself, "I've never had an afternoon quite like this. It just seems like everywhere we go there's such fruit, power, fulfillment—things are happening today!"

A moment or so later, I whispered, "Lord, why is this?"

The answer came almost immediately, a deep impression within my spirit: *Because there are two of you out together.*

I was used to going out alone, so I thought, "Well, what difference does that make?" And the Lord impressed my heart with this very simple truth: *When two of My people join in a spirit of love, they command great power. Regardless of how many of the adversary there are, none of them is in unity with another; they're only under authority, but without harmony. I have sent you in the name of an authority greater than any authority on their side that you will encounter. And when there are two of you, your agreement always overwhelms them, not only by the authority present with you, but because the two of you together face every single one of them alone. They are isolated by their bitterness and rebellion. They have no unity; when there are two of you, you always outnumber them!*

PERSONAL CASUALTIES

> In the fourteenth year Chedorlaomer and the kings that were with him came and attacked the Rephaim in Ashteroth Karnaim, the Zuzim in Ham, the Emim in Shaveh Kiriathaim, and the Horites in their mountain of Seir, as far as El Paran, which is by the wilderness. Then they turned back and came to En Mishpat (that is, Kadesh), and attacked all the country of the Amalekites, and also the Amorites who dwelt in Hazezon Tamar.
>
> And the king of Sodom, the king of Gomorrah, the king of Admah, the king of Zeboiim, and the king of Bela (that is, Zoar) went out and joined together in battle in the Valley of Siddim against Chedor-

> laomer king of Elam, Tidal king of nations, Amraphel king of Shinar, and Arioch king of Ellasar; four kings against five. (Genesis 14:5–9)

In the midst of the sweeping international conflict depicted in Genesis 14, two familiar names appear.

Abraham and Lot. Uncle and nephew.

When he initially heard of the warfare taking place in the land, Abraham may have shrugged and said, "Well, so there's another war. That's too bad, but what does it have to do with me? It really doesn't concern me and mine."

But then he heard news that *did* concern him very much. Suddenly that "distant" war came very close to home.

> Now the Valley of Siddim was full of asphalt pits; and the kings of Sodom and Gomorrah fled; some fell there, and the remainder fled to the mountains. Then they took all the goods of Sodom and Gomorrah, and all their provisions, and went their way. They also took Lot, Abram's brother's son who dwelt in Sodom, and his goods, and departed.
>
> Then one who had escaped came and told Abram the Hebrew, for he dwelt by the terebinth trees of Mamre. (14:10–13)

Friend, none of us who is connected in some way with even one victim of the present spiritual struggle—and we *all* are—can afford to remain neutral about the conflict. As believers we are automatically involved. The question becomes: How do we do battle in this perpetual war? We could just stand aside, and say, "Well, this struggle was going on before I was born and will continue after I die. Who am I against those great shadowy armies? What do I have to do with a warfare I can't even see?"

But what did Abraham do? He was in the proximity of huge warring armies, with many thousands of warriors. And the ones who took Lot were already victorious and marching off in triumph!

So Abraham looked around him to take inventory...and what did he have? How did he match up against a conquering force of allied armies?

In fact, he matched up quite well.

PREPARING TO DO BATTLE

> Now when Abraham heard that his [relative] was taken captive, he armed his three hundred and eighteen trained servants who were born in his own house, and went in pursuit as far as Dan. (14:14)

When you're preparing for battle, as Abraham was, the first thing you do is decide that the sweep of great events around does not indicate your insignificance. On the contrary, it underscores your *strategic importance!* Your role as God's agent behind enemy lines is vital.

In Abraham's case, who would enter the conflict and rescue the loved ones who had been captured?

There was nobody else.

There was no U.N. No Geneva Convention. No World Court. No Red Cross. No Amnesty International. If Abraham didn't rise up and at the risk of life and limb go after Lot and his family, no one would. Ever. Abraham would live for the rest of his days with the knowledge that his brother's son and family were enslaved to a cruel enemy. But what were the logical prospects for a rescue mission? It was obviously going to take more than the arm of man to succeed. Nevertheless the participation of that man, *God's* man, was still critical.

There were thousands of men in those retreating armies. And what kind of forces could Abraham muster? *Three hundred eighteen household servants.* What was that? It was like a Boy Scout troop compared to the enemy's numbers. But there was no hesitation. He armed his men and marched out, double time.

And where was Abraham placing his confidence as he marched out? In his conscript company of former camel tenders and baggage handlers? In his own prowess as a general of armies? *Don't bet on it!* Abraham was an altar builder, a man in touch with heaven, a man who had been walking in the will of God for years now. He left home and roots and everything familiar back in Ur to follow the voice of the Lord. He left a temporary but very comfortable camping spot in Haran to continue on to a land he'd never seen. He'd watched God's hand rescue him from his own fear and folly in Egypt and bring him back to Canaan with more wealth than he'd ever had before. He'd heard God's promise again and again; the land would be his; his own descendants would inherit it.

Abraham had some history with God. They had a track record together. He'd seen God's faithfulness again and again. Why *wouldn't* he trust God to help him in this new crisis? He took immediate steps to rescue his family from the hand of the enemy. As we consider these steps, we gain insight into our own need for preparation in the war that surges around us.

Arm yourself

> When Abram heard that his [relative] was taken captive, he armed his three hundred and eighteen trained servants who were born in his own house, and went in pursuit. (14:14)

The first thing you do is arm yourself. None of us should launch into spiritual battle ignorantly, blindly, foolishly, exuberantly, zealously—without wisdom. Don't wander onto the battlefield in a baseball cap, T-shirt, and Bermuda shorts. Arm yourself! The Bible provides all the information we need about dressing for battle.

> Finally, be strong in the Lord and in his mighty power. Put on the full armor of God so that you can take your stand against the devil's schemes. (Ephesians 6:10–11, NIV)

Now there's a direct command if you're ever going to hear one. Why be strong in the Lord and strap on the armor of God?

So you can *stand.*

> So use every piece of God's armor to resist the enemy whenever he attacks, and when it is all over, you will still be standing up. (Ephesians 6:13, TLB)

What a beautiful image. After the battle has been fought and the dust has settled and the smoke has rolled away, God's warrior will still be standing. I love that picture. You go into battle, and after all the shooting and shouting, after all the bomb blasts, machine-gun fire, and artillery salvoes, when the smoke drifts away, someone says, "Where is he? Ah, there he is—still standing, holding his ground." That will be the outcome, says the Lord, for those who are properly armed.

Strive for likemindedness

First Peter 4:1 is an interesting verse: "Since Christ suffered for us in the flesh, arm yourselves also with the same mind." When I read this verse, I hear Peter urging us to join others who share the same attitude—the very mind-set of Jesus Christ who took His stand against Satan and suffered for our sins.

Within His greater, universal body, the Church, I believe the Lord raises up people in family groups, in local bodies. These groups don't shut out other families—no more than my family shuts out other families in the physical dimension. But along with our spiritual relationship, in a local body of believers we also have a friendship, a family relationship. A *family* meets at The Church On The Way, the local fellowship where I pastor. But just blocks away, there are other church families. And down the road are many, many more. We're all part of the larger family of God, but there are individual families within that larger family, meeting in different places.

We need to foster the unity, the interrelatedness, of those families. But at the same time, when it comes to doing spiritual battle, it is appropriate that you recognize your own household in a special way.

Notice what Abraham did. "He armed his trained servants, *born in his own house.*" These were people who understood one another's temperament. They thought along the same lines. They knew each other's strengths and weaknesses and quirks. When Abraham received the bad news, he didn't go out and whip up a posse. He took along only those born in his own house. He said, "For this operation, I want only those who understand how we operate." Together, they armed themselves and went out.

Had they trained in battle techniques together through the years? Had they prepared themselves for this sort of situation? The Bible doesn't say. There must have been something of an armory in Abraham's little caravan because Scripture says they went out armed. It also tells us that these servants were *trained* and that they moved out as a body. There wasn't a single "conscientious objector" in the bunch. They *all* went on this operation.

When writing to the Philippians, the apostle Paul repeatedly emphasizes the same principle implied in 1 Peter 4:1.

> Only let your conduct be worthy of the gospel of Christ, so that whether I come and see you or am absent, I may hear of your affairs, that you stand fast in one spirit, with one mind striving together for the faith of the gospel, and not in any way terrified by your adversaries. (Philippians 1:27–28)

Stand fast in one spirit, strive together with one mind, and in *nothing* be terrified by the opposition. Paul goes on to say:

> Let nothing be done through selfish ambition or conceit, but in lowliness of mind let each esteem others better than himself.... Let this mind be in you which was also in Christ Jesus. (Philippians 2:3, 5)

A few verses later, the apostle referred to Timothy and said: "For I have no one like-minded, who will sincerely care for your state" (v. 20). Paul was saying that he needed Timothy to be a part of his spiritual ministry because Timothy thought just like him and would help the Philippians grow in *their* likemindedness.

And again, in chapter 4, verse 2, we read: "I implore Euodia and I implore Syntyche to *be of the same mind in the Lord.*"

Be of the same mind. *It may be the difference between spiritual victory and spiritual defeat!* If a group of believers are going to labor together and be successful in battle together against a common enemy—the powers of darkness—they must think the same way...hold certain principles in common...share many values...enjoy a high degree of unity. People who are "born of the same house" really care for one another.

Now, even though Lot wasn't of the house of Abraham any longer, Lot and Abraham had strong blood ties. And when Abraham heard that Lot had been captured, he said, "We're going after that boy. We're going to fetch him home. He's kin!" And so Abraham and his household servants went out together to seek the rescue of one related by blood.

There are two fundamental truths here, I think. The first relates to those of us who are of the same house: *We need to learn how to agree together in the Lord.* The Bible speaks of how "two [shall] put ten thousand to flight" (Deuteronomy 32:30). But first there must be agreement. Once that agreement is achieved...well, you do the math. If two like-minded warriors shall put ten thousand to flight, what will a hundred do? How about a thousand? That's Holy Spirit manpower, the Lord entering into human flesh and saying, "Tear down the strongholds. Go in power."

But there's a second truth. *Our warfare against hell needs to be as united and zealous for other members of Christ's body as it is for those of our own immediate circle.* Why? Because even if we don't live in the same "house," we're still all bought by the same Blood! We have Blood-ties through Christ's Cross, and we need to support one another.

Pray for an effective battle strategy

> [Abraham] divided his forces against them by night, and he and his servants attacked them and pursued them as far as Hobah, which is north of Damascus. (Genesis 14:15)

Abraham and his small band of warriors pursued the adversary to Dan, in the north of Canaan, and then followed them on to Hobah. So there are two pursuits here: He pursued them to Dan and pursued them to Hobah. Now, that first pursuit amounted to chasing them to simply *find out where they were*.

This illustrates another principle of spiritual warfare: You don't pursue your foe arbitrarily or aimlessly; *you go to the point where the enemy is*. You identify the hot spots of enemy activity. And the key to determining those potential battle grounds is effective, fervent prayer.

Did you know there's a lot of meaningless prayer spoken in the church today? And it's uttered in the name of Jesus! The apostle Paul said, "I do not fight like a man beating the air" (1 Corinthians 9:26, NIV). In other words, "I don't want to just shadowbox; I want my punches to count!" Let's *target* our prayers. Let's avoid being people who, however enthusiastic, still just beat the air in prayer. They aren't engaged in spiritual warfare because they pray abstractly. To avoid shadowboxing, accomplishing little or nothing, we have a real need for spiritual discernment, and that is derived by two means: waiting on God for direction (Psalm 18:32–34), and praying in the Spirit with power (Ephesians 6:12, 18).

When we read how Abraham pursued them to Dan, don't mistakenly think this means he *chased* them to Dan. No. He went there and then found out where they were camped. He *located* his adversary there. He didn't just go tromping around at random, making loud noises across the land. Abraham's band was an elite strike force. He led them to victory by zeroing in on those he pursued. Similarly, in prayer warfare, you and I need to ask the Holy Spirit to show us where to locate the enemy activity in and around our lives, our communities, and our circumstances. We need to ask Him to show us where to confront our adversary most effectively.

After Abraham located the kidnappers, "He divided his forces against them by night, and he and his servants attacked them" (Genesis 14:15). I get so excited when I read that! They attacked in the middle of the night. Do you know what that suggests to me? Night, darkness, is the very element that encompasses our adversary—but it doesn't get in the way of our coming against him! Why? Because we're children of the day! Wherever we go, there's enough light for us to move in victory and triumph. The enemy is swathed in his own blackness, but that doesn't hinder us at all. The Bible says, "The light still shines in the darkness, and the darkness has never put it out" (John 1:5, PHILLIPS). Hallelujah!

So Abraham came by night and struck them like summer lightning, and the enemy forces scattered in panic. Scripture tells us that "he pursued them as far as Hobah." This time he was running them down, and he didn't stop until he cornered them and destroyed them in battle.

VICTORY GROUND

I've often found there are insights inherent in the historical accounts the Bible reports. In particular, I see more-than-accidental significance in the *names* of the places and people in the stories. Focus with me for a moment on two of the place names found in Genesis 14.

Consider this: The name Dan means "judge" or "judgment," and the name Hobah carries the idea of a secret, private place of rest. I find this so interesting because Abraham actually *did* pursue his enemies *first* to Dan; that is to the judge (God the deliverer) or to the judgment (the exacting of justice). His second and concluding strike (Hobah) resulted in a "rest" from battle. I think these ideas intensify a principle. Listen loved one, *we will never conquer the enemy, our adversary, in our own strength.*

Yes, we *do* need to prepare ourselves for battle, putting on the armor of God. Yes, we *do* need to be like-minded as we strive together in this warfare. And yes, we *do* need an effective battle strategy that comes to us through long seasons of prayer. All of these elements are needed for spiritual battle. But when it finally comes to smiting the enemy, our victory will be won only by bringing him to the ultimate place of true judgment: the Cross. We drive the Adversary to Calvary. That's what prayer warfare is, bringing every issue generated by sin, self, or Satan and all his cohorts, to the place where the blood of Jesus Christ was spilled, to the place where the forces of darkness were and are vanquished.

I often hear people say something like, "Satan, I bind you," and that has its place. But I'll tell you something that'll get him twice as fast: *Get him on Calvary ground.* Confront him with the Cross of Christ and the Blood of Christ. Because where the Blood was shed, *that* is where the power of the enemy was broken. That's where the head of the serpent was smitten (Genesis 3:15).

In Colossians 2:14–15, we read that at the Cross an open spectacle was made of the powers of darkness, and those evil princes were torn down. Just listen to this!

> He has forgiven you all your sins: he has utterly wiped out the written evidence of broken commandments which always hung over our heads, and has completely annulled it by nailing it to the cross. And then, having drawn the sting of all the powers and authorities ranged against us, he exposed them, shattered, empty and defeated, in his own triumphant victory! (PHILLIPS)

Bring your foe to the place of judgment, and then watch him and his comrades scatter and run. But don't stop there. Chase him down, and don't stop the pursuit until the issue you've brought to the Cross—that matter which created the conflict, which brought the bondage—has been settled. It is then you'll enter into a place of secret rest—your "Hobah."

Learn this, please: Pursuing God's will for our victory means pursuing each battle until the enemy is vanquished. Don't stop until the enemy is smitten with the Cross's judgment. Don't stop until a perfect rest is achieved in your soul. Those are basic principles of warfare, if you're going to do battle in the will of God.

> So he brought back all the goods, and also brought back his [nephew] Lot and his goods, as well as the women and the people. And the king of Sodom went out to meet him at the Valley of Shaveh (that is, the King's Valley), after his return from the defeat of Chedorlaomer and the kings who were with him.
>
> Then Melchizedek king of Salem brought out bread and wine; he was the priest of God Most High. (Genesis 14:16–18)

It's interesting to make a parallel study of these two kings. It's not difficult to say the king of Sodom literally represents the "king of hell," not only because of the evil present there but also because the name Sodom actually translates "burnt" or "scorched," (probably because of the arid, bitterly hot desert region). So we read how the king of Sodom, the leader of a hell-bent city that would later be destroyed by fire, went out to meet Abraham, a conqueror through faith in God.

Almost simultaneously, from another city nearby, the king of Salem appears, approaching Abraham. Salem, in this text, is known to be the ancient site of Jerusalem and was the dwelling of an early priest who worshiped "the Most High God" and rejected the idolatrous, demon-inspired worship of the surrounding cultures. This priest had preceded the Levitical priesthood; Melchizedek is mentioned in the Book of Hebrews as a direct type, or advance picture, of Jesus Himself! So we see a confrontation in Abraham's experience. In the wake of victory, a challenge and a choice. On the one hand he is approached by the king of evil—Satan himself as it were; while on the other hand, Melchizedek approaches him—a "priest of the Most High God" and a picture of the Son of God Himself.

CHOOSE THE SPIRITUAL OVER THE MATERIAL

Here is another valuable lesson for all who seek to pursue the will of God. *You will never gain a spiritual victory but that you will instantly be called upon to face a choice at a practical level,* one which will test the very fabric of the triumph gained. Gain a spiritual victory, and you will undoubtedly face a practical decision. As you do, the Adversary will always employ maximum stealth in order to conceal his real effort...that of neutralizing your recent triumph over him by gaining a different sort of hold in your life.

Notice the smooth, silky subtlety of the king of Sodom's approach: "Now the king of Sodom said to Abram, 'Give me the persons, and take the goods for yourself'" (14:21).

In other words, "Look, you can have all the plunder, just give me the people." That's so very like Satan! "I'll give you anything—just let me control people!"

But Abraham was prepared in advance for Sodom's king. He had just met with Melchizedek, whose name literally means "the prince or King of peace" And please look at this incredible encounter: What does Melchizedek—this Old Testament picture of Jesus—bring to that meeting? Bread and wine. Can you believe it? Here we are, twenty-two hundred years before Christ, looking at a virtual painting of Jesus that is so completely consistent with what we know of our incarnated Savior. Melchizedek comes with bread and wine, the very portrait of the commemoration of the Lord's supper and of His death on the Cross. Moreover, it's a way to note that Jesus would die on that Cross and bring conclusion and defeat to the armies of hell *just a few short miles from where Abraham met with Melchizedek* to worship.

And Abraham *did* worship. He "lifted up his hands"—a biblical expression demonstrating a pledge and commitment of one's whole being in praise, in blessing, and in surrender. He worshiped the Lord, God Most High, and later, when the king of Sodom approached him, he was ready.

> Abram said to the king of Sodom, "I have raised my hand to the LORD, God Most High, the Possessor of heaven and earth, that I will take nothing, from a thread to a sandal strap, and that I will not take anything that is yours, lest you should say, 'I have made Abram rich.'" (14:22–23)

Abraham countered the pagan king's offer with a declaration of his commitment: "I've already made my choice. I've lifted up my hand to the Most High God, the Creator and Lord of all. You're not going to make me rich on your terms. I'm going the Lord's way."

AFTER VICTORY...ON YOUR GUARD!

Spiritual warfare *will* culminate in victory when we war in the will of God. But you will always find that *after* the victory there will be another subtle approach of the enemy—in a very different sort of attack.

It's comparatively easy to think about the big spiritual battles of life. We gear ourselves up for the big confrontations, complete with spiritual fireworks, battle cries, explosions, blood flowing, and all the drama. Then, when we prevail through the power of Christ, how easy it is to walk away, dusting off our hands and, with uninterested carelessness, *immediately let down our guard.*

That is an instant of grave spiritual danger.

While we're wrapping up with our victory lap, waving at the cheering crowds, the serpent slithers in again from a totally unexpected angle. While we're celebrating and feeling good about the outcome of the great battle, the enemy immediately sets to work contriving another—and usually very different—sort of trap. It's oh-too-easy to fall flat on our faces right after we have won a victory and our face is aglow with joy.

Be on the lookout for it. When we walk with God, He will help us identify and defeat that attack too. How? I suggest it will be by the same means which paved the pathway to Abraham's overcoming. Notice, after defeating huge enemy armies, he soon faced the seductive wiles of a so-called friend. How did he do it? Answer: He did it by means of what came *in between* those two attacks:

Worship.

Abraham was in the presence of God's King. And having lifted up his hands to God Most High—having honored God's high priest—he was equipped for the second, more subtle attack.

Let's follow his example, and, in the will of God, we'll be ready too. We'll be ready for victories and ready to sustain those victories, moving on from triumph to triumph.

CHAPTER FIVE

Learning to Walk in the Dark

> After these things the word of the LORD came to Abram in a vision, saying, "Do not be afraid, Abram. I am your shield, your exceedingly great reward." But Abram said, "Lord GOD, what will You give me, seeing I go childless, and the heir of my house is Eliezer of Damascus?" Then Abram said, "Look, You have given me no offspring; indeed one born in my house is my heir!" (Genesis 15:1–3)

Genesis 15 speaks of a point in your life and mine when only a deeper manifestation of the Person and heart of the Lord will enable us to understand His personal way with us and His plans for us.

We can never keep growing in the Lord on the strength of past experiences. But at the same time, remember this: Moving *forward* in the will of God means testing and challenge. A new revelation of Himself usually is accompanied by a corresponding obstacle...a difficulty...a darkness...that is designed to strengthen the core of our faith. There are no cheap price tags on "going deeper with God."

I frequently encounter believers who speak of glorious past experiences with the Lord. They will describe great blessings and miracles of God's grace and power but then relate coming to a place in their lives when the "blessings spigot" seemed to close off—and remain closed. The good times with the Lord seemed to be replaced by a season of trials, heartaches, or perplexities. They will explain how they couldn't see beyond the trial at the time, so at that juncture had no notion of the eventual new dimension of grace that was being ushered in.

They entered a season of darkness. The psalmist describes experiencing something similar. Slumped in some dark, lonely corner and weighed down with anxieties and burdens, he penned these words:

> My tears have been my food day and night,
> while men say to me all day long,
> "Where is your God?"
> These things I remember as I pour out my soul:
> how I used to go with the multitude,
> leading the procession to the house of God,
> with shouts of joy and thanksgiving
> among the festive throng....
> My soul is downcast within me;
> therefore I will remember you from the land of the Jordan,
> the heights of Hermon—from Mount Mizar.
>
> (Psalm 42:3–4, 6, NIV)

The psalmist is thinking about the "good old days" when God seemed near and dear, when life was exciting, when believing men and women surrounded him, and when they worshiped and sang praises to the Lord together. He's remembering some wonderful places and wonderful moments—exhilarating mountaintops—when he met with the Lord and everything in life seemed clear and bright as a summer morning.

We have similar laments when we enter those inevitable dark tunnels in the will of God. Perhaps we've even said words such as these...

"I guess the Lord's through with me."

"Something's wrong. God isn't happy with me anymore."

"God's gotten so busy He's forgotten about me."

"God has abandoned me to the devil."

"I feel so overwhelmed I'm almost beside myself!"

The truth is, though, there are times when the Lord allows His people to walk in the dark. He knows exactly where they are at every moment along the way; He never abandons or loses track of His children.

No, out of love He allows us to enter the darkness in order to bring us to a place where we must admit, "I don't know where I am or where I'm going." The only way He can ready us to receive the next thing He plans to teach us is by helping us understand that we don't have all the answers—or even very many of them. He reminds us that we need to know things only God can reveal to us. So He lets us enter the darkness for a season so that we have an opportunity to grow.

We need to learn how to see in the dark, how to walk in the will of God during the sunless days of pain and troubles, pushing through the difficulties to the glory of new understanding and renewed blessing beyond.

Abraham had several "journeys into darkness" in his lifetime. As a matter of fact, his very first step out of the city limits of Ur—heading toward a mysterious land he had never seen—was a step into darkness. He had to learn to walk by faith. He had to learn to live a day at a time, leaning on God's provision, protection, and guidance. Through it all, he came to understand that what had seemed like darkness was in reality a path leading to a light greater than he had ever known.

QUESTIONS OF A SUBMISSIVE HEART

And behold, the word of the LORD came to him, saying, "This one shall not be your heir, but one who will come from your own body

> shall be your heir." Then He brought him outside and said, "Look now toward heaven, and count the stars if you are able to number them." And He said to him, "So shall your descendants be." And he believed in the LORD, and He accounted it to him for righteousness.
>
> Then He said to him, "I am the LORD, who brought you out of Ur of the Chaldeans, to give you this land to inherit it." And he said, "Lord GOD, how shall I know that I will inherit it?" (Genesis 15:4–8)

Abraham asked two basic questions in this chapter:

> *"Lord, what will You give me?"* (v. 2), and
> *"Lord, how shall I know that I will inherit?"* (v. 8).

Abraham wasn't being irreverent or demanding with these questions. Anyone who from a full heart can address God as Master, Lord, and Commander of Life—as Abraham did—has every right to ask such things. He wasn't looking to argue with God; he was looking for wisdom. Abraham's questions were the honest queries of a submitted heart that still longed for answers. Submission doesn't teach everything; it just prepares us to be taught and to receive instruction in the will of God.

In the last chapter we read how Abraham steadfastly refused the goods and booty offered him as a reward by the king of Sodom. He told the pagan king, "I will take nothing, from a thread to a sandal strap,...I will not take anything that is yours, lest you should say, 'I have made Abram rich'" (Genesis 14:23).

How much did Abraham give up in that determination? We have no idea what the spoils of those great battles may have been, but it would have been no small chunk of change. It probably amounted to a great fortune. But he spurned that offer, not wanting to be beholden or obligated in any way to a godless earthly ruler. He chose instead to honor and fully trust his God, "the Possessor of heaven and earth."

"I don't need special favors from you," he told the king. "I don't want your silver or your gold, your cattle or your slaves. I serve the Lord of all—the One who possesses everything! He is fully able to meet my needs."

It was after all this had taken place that the Lord appeared to Abraham and said, in effect, "You've chosen well. Don't concern yourself about this decision, and don't be afraid. I am your shield! I am your great reward. I will keep My covenant with you."

Abraham, who had committed himself to God's way at great personal cost, came back with his questions: "Lord, what *will* You give me? You see my situation. What will You do for me?"

I don't believe it's as if Abraham were saying, "Yeah, right, God; promises, promises, always promises, but what's in it for me right now?" I don't think his posture toward the Lord was like that at all. But I do think he experienced something very human, common to all of us from time to time when the Lord doesn't seem to be making good on promises we believe He has given us. I think he was confused and unsure about what was coming next. He simply wanted to *know*.

Abraham was doing what we all do at times: With a pure heart he questioned God when he wasn't able to understand what was happening in his life. Sometimes when life throws us a curve, or maybe a whole flurry of them, we experience sentiments similar to this...

"Lord, You promised so and so, and I even heard You speaking to my heart..." or *"I read this in the Word and You seemed to say it was something for me..."* or *"The Spirit of God prompted me with this thought, and I thought I understood this thing about my life and my future, but Lord, I don't see anything happening. It puzzles me. Did I make a mistake? Is something wrong with me?"*

If relief for our distress and answers to our prayers take more than two weeks, you and I tend to think we're undergoing an enormous test of faith. Many of us would profit by going back and helping Noah build the ark for a hundred years. Noah just went about his business, hammering nails, slopping pitch, and punching that old time clock *for a century*, not seeing any evidence that what he believed would happen was taking place.

But he hung in there through those long, dry years. And the rains came, just as God had said. Boy, did they come!

I remember so well the testimony of a woman who had believed the Lord would save her husband after she herself accepted Christ. He finally did receive the Lord—two weeks before he died. And that was *forty years* after *her* conversion. She prayed for her man and trusted the Lord for his salvation for forty years.

The Lord *does* get the job done...but not necessarily on our timetable.

TRAIN YOUR FOCUS ON HIM

I think one of the principal things going on in this mysterious chapter of Genesis, aside from the revelation God delivers to Abraham, is this: The Lord is focusing Abraham's attention on Himself: "*I* am your shield. *I* am your great reward." Friend, when the Lord becomes to you the fountain of everything meaningful in life, you will never be disappointed, no matter what happens or doesn't happen on your schedule or wish list. An abiding stability and peace come into your life when you realize you're on unshakable territory with the Lord Himself.

But Abraham hadn't found this abiding peace yet.

He said, "Lord GOD, what will You give me, seeing I go childless, and the heir of my house is Eliezer of Damascus?... Look, You have given me no offspring" (15:2–3). God had promised Abraham heirs in chapter 12, verse 7 and chapter 13, verse 16. But nothing was happening. And it began to look more and more as if nothing *would* happen.

Why does Abraham bring up Eliezer? I really think he is saying—and not as a complaint—"Lord, the only possible heir I see in this house is my servant Eliezer. You haven't given me any children, Sarah and I aren't getting any younger, and it's not working out the way I thought it would. Is there some kind of 'spiritual' answer to this that I just don't see? Is there an interpretation or a special spin on these words I don't understand? Is Eliezer the answer? Is he the one You really meant?"

But the Lord immediately responds, in verse 4, "This one shall not be your heir, but one who will come from your own body shall be your heir."

God didn't want his servant to settle for anything less than a miracle. As with Abraham, many of us are all too ready to accept a spiritualization of the Lord's word to us, or some watered down "answer" that misses His full intent (and is really no answer at all). We often conclude, "Well, I guess what He *really* means is..." But when the Lord declares Himself on a definite point, *that's exactly what He will do*. He will deliver the goods as promised, possibly not in the way we imagined but always to the full dimension He has described. He knows what He's said, and He means what He says.

Indeed, loved one, the Lord will remain faithful to His word. So don't stop short of keeping patience in awaiting His full promise. Don't settle for less than what He wants to accomplish in and through your life.

IN THE DARKNESS, LOOK FOR STARS OF PROMISE

I love the ensuing interchange between the Lord and Abraham in verses 3 and 5.

> Abraham had said to God, "Look, You have given me no offspring!"
> The Lord responded, "No, *you* come and look!"

And God walked him out under the night sky. What an awesome moment that must have been! Out under the stars with the Lord of the universe. Out under the great vault of heaven with the very One who formed the galaxies and sent them spinning into the incomprehensible depths of space.

It was as if the Lord was saying, "You refused the rewards of Sodom to serve Me, Abraham? You lifted up your hand to the Possessor of heaven and earth? Very well, then, I want to fill your eyes and fill your heart with something. I am your reward, My son, and I am able to make your descendants as numerous as those stars that fill the sky."

I love the phrase in the text that says, "He brought him outside and said, 'Now look toward heaven.'" He took him out of the tent and away from the little campfires. He led him up on a little hill and said, "*Now* look."

And Abraham looked.

This was a time in our world when night was truly night. Not a single streetlight, electric bulb, car headlight, or bit of flashing neon could be found on the whole earth. No airplanes or jets or satellites winked across the sky. As Abraham stood there in inky darkness, the starry expanse must have been stunning. The great Milky Way must have cut a swath across the heavens like a highway of diamonds. And I wonder...did the Lord show him stars beyond stars we can see with the naked eye? Did He show him galaxies beyond galaxies, as He certainly would have been able to do?

The Bible doesn't say.

But whatever the Lord showed him, it was enough.

Recall that the Lord told Abraham in Genesis 13:16, "I will make your descendants as the dust of the earth." But that may have been too bewildering for Abraham to imagine. So the Master Teacher took him for a walk under the stars and said, "Just look up, and you'll see what I mean."

And there follows that beautiful declaration in verse 5: "'Look now toward heaven, and count the stars if you are able to number them.' And He said to him, 'So shall your descendants be.'" Abraham, who had been wrestling with these revelations and trying to grasp something that didn't really seem possible, is told, "Look! Lift up your eyes, child, and begin to see."

And in that moment, with his face upturned toward heaven, something happened in his heart.

> *And he believed in the LORD, and He accounted it to him for righteousness.* (Genesis 15:6)

It is this very verse in Scripture upon which the primary argument of the Book of Galatians and the Book of Romans turns. It paves the way to understanding faith as the sole means for being declared righteous in God's sight. And it provides the grid undergirding the transition period that would allow expansion to give place to the complete church, as God conceived it—a people in Christ, who would be neither Jew nor Gentile, male nor female, slave nor free. It anticipates the time when the Lord would explode the idea that faith is limited to a single race or nationality, and open up the promise of eternity with the Lord to all mankind...even you and me.

The Lord had said to his servant, "In the midst of your darkness, look up toward heaven, and there you will see the stars of promise."

Abraham believed the Lord...and took a giant leap in the will of God.

WALKING IN THE DARK

When you ask, "Lord, what are You going to give me?" He will always give you His word. And He will back up His word with Himself. Why? Because He wants you to *know* Him, to *grow* in Him, to have your *focus* on Him. "I am your shield and your exceedingly great reward."

The way you learn to walk in the dark

—when you can't see your hand in front of your face

—when the Lord's way seems a dead-end street

—when all His promises seem out of reach is to come right back to Him again and say, "Lord, I just don't understand. Please show me Your heart in this, for I am depending on You alone." Or as David wrote: "Lead me in Your truth and teach me, for You are the God of my salvation; on You I wait all the day" (Psalm 25:5).

I am persuaded He will do for you what He has done for others. He will draw you to Himself and so catch you up in Himself that you will know with certainty that God will not fail you. Will He take you for a walk under the stars? He may, but then again, He has many ways of showing You His faithfulness and His plans as you wait on Him.

But the question is, after He shows you, will you believe?

"And [Abraham] believed in the LORD; and He accounted it to him for righteousness."

NEW REVELATIONS...AND NEW TESTS

> He said to him, "Bring Me a three-year-old heifer, a three-year-old female goat, a three-year-old ram, a turtledove, and a young pigeon." Then he brought all these to Him and cut them in two, down the middle, and placed each piece opposite the other; but he did not cut the birds in two. And when the vultures came down on the carcasses, Abram drove them away.
>
> Now when the sun was going down, a deep sleep fell upon Abram; and behold, horror and great darkness fell upon him. Then He said to Abram: "Know certainly that your descendants will be strangers in a land that is not theirs, and will serve them, and they will afflict them four hundred years. And also the nation whom they serve I will judge; afterward they shall come out with great possessions. Now as for you, you shall go to your fathers in peace; you shall be buried at a good old age. But in the fourth generation they shall return here, for the iniquity of the Amorites is not yet complete."
>
> And it came to pass, when the sun went down and it was dark, that behold, there appeared a smoking oven and a burning torch that passed between those pieces. On the same day the LORD made a covenant with Abram, saying: "To your descendants I have given this land, from the river of Egypt to the great river, the River Euphrates." (Genesis 15:9–18)

The fire of the Lord moved through the pieces of the sacrifice.

The manifest presence of God was in that place. The Spirit of the Lord was present in the fire, just as He was in the fire which came down upon Elijah's sacrifice (1 Kings 18), and in the fire that came out from the presence of the Lord and consumed Nadab and Abihu, the sons of Aaron, when they offered "profane fire" to the Lord (Leviticus 10). This same fire of God made up the pillar of fire that led God's people as they fled slavery in Egypt (Exodus 13). That was the fire that came and consumed Abraham's sacrifice.

Was this Abraham's first blood sacrifice to the Lord? I've often wondered. Nowhere before this is it mentioned that Abraham offered a sacrifice. We know he raised altars several times, and you could easily assume he offered sacrifices on those altars. But I am inclined to believe he raised those altars as simple monuments to the Lord where he called upon the name of the Lord.

At God's command, Abraham had to deal with the blood of sacrifice. He learned that sacrifice is central to God's program of walking with man. How does a holy God fulfill His promises to sinful men and women? He works through sacrifice. Although Abraham couldn't have known it, animal sacrifices pointed the way toward the perfect sacrifice God Himself would make on Calvary, Jesus Christ.

Abraham wanted to know specific details about his own life and future—how things would work out for him. God gave him some of those details, but He also gave him more than he asked. He revealed *Himself* to Abraham. He revealed His program for the salvation of men that would culminate in the shedding of blood. The slain, broken animals were a picture of God's own slain, broken Son who would give His life for the salvation of the world.

In Rembrandt's famous painting "Descent from the Cross," the painter depicts the limp, lifeless body of Jesus being lowered from a bloody cross. Not everyone realizes it, but Rembrandt painted himself into that dark, gloomy scene. He is depicted as a young man in blue, up on a ladder, gripping the Lord's arm as His body is gently lowered into waiting hands below.

Through this, the painter wished to show that all men of all times are responsible for the death of Christ. We all have blood on our hands.

In the Old Testament, animal sacrifice was a forecast of that truth.

> And when the vultures came down on the carcasses, Abram drove them away. Now when the sun was going down, a deep sleep fell upon Abram; and behold, horror and great darkness fell upon him. (15:11–12)

It was a truly awesome, holy moment. God would show things to his servant He had never shown anyone before. But as Abraham was waiting there by the sacrifice to meet the Lord, the fowls descended; the vultures came to rip and tear and steal. In several New Testament parables, the fowls of the air symbolize the working of the powers of darkness.

The fact is, Satan opposes any significant new connection between God and His children. Any effort to step into a deeper, more profound aspect of God's working in your life will bring vultures from the pit, who will come to tear and despoil and devour.

Abraham—though standing alone in the darkness—diligently beat those things away.

Loved one, once you make a commitment in faith, don't ever imagine Satan won't test that commitment! When you expose yourself by choosing to trust God, Satan *will* sweep down and try to destroy what the Lord is attempting to produce in your life.

How should you deal with this enemy? As soon as he comes, you immediately need to rise up and *resist* him. As James wrote: "Resist the devil and he will flee from you" (James 4:7). Abraham beat the carrion birds away and protected the sacrifice. And that, dear friend, is our responsibility too.

I constantly hear people say they've "really been plagued by the devil lately." But I would surely love to hear a lot more people say, "The devil's been plaguing me, but I have begun to stand up and sweep back at him! I am *resist-*

ing him." I have an idea that if we would rise up, stand tall, and *move,* then we would find that Satan is not as formidable an adversary as many of us think. Yes, he is a mighty enemy. But I'm telling you, when you get on your feet and begin to move in the power of Christ, those vultures will scatter. If we just sit back, wring our hands, and say, "Oh, Satan's just been tormenting me so…" we're easy pickings! Passive or negative responses block our steps forward in the will of God, and His larger plans for us will never get off the ground. This will never be because the Father is unfaithful but only because we haven't risen as His sons and daughters to declare our family inheritance in the face of the Enemy.

So, get up and lay it on him! Rise up in the name of Jesus! Take the blood of the Cross and hold it before him. He *will* flee. He *must!*

After Abraham defended the sacrifice, night fell, and he entered into what the Scripture calls "a horror and great darkness." There will be black times ahead for us, too, my brother or sister. As we advance in the will of God, they are certain to come. And when you face one of those periods, I wish I could be there with you, holding your hand. I've experienced some of those times when I couldn't see *anything*. There didn't seem to be any light anywhere.

Abraham suddenly felt fathoms deep under a black sea.

But what was the first thing Abraham heard in this deep darkness? *The voice of the Lord!* God was there with him, and He began to reveal glimpses of the future to Abraham. He said, to paraphrase, "Now I am going to explain to you something about My timing, Abraham. I am going to keep My promise to you, but it's not going to work out in the manner you imagined. It's not going to happen the way you've tried to rationalize that it might with Eliezer. It's not going to move along lines you have thought on your own. There is so much more involved than you know. Abraham, I'm not only dealing with you; there are many other people under My watchful eye. Recognize this: My dealing with you is necessarily going at a pace that incorporates the flow of my dealings with other nations and peoples."

Dear child of God, the truth is, none of us lives or dies unto ourselves. If you were to say, "Lord, I want thus and so to happen, and I want it to happen *now*" and He were to give it to you "right now," it could block or damage what the Lord wants to work out in two hundred thousand other lives! One of the grand reasons we must trust the Lord's timing is because there is so great an interweaving in what He is doing in *our* lives with what He is doing in other lives.

THE LORD DELIVERS MORE THAN WE EXPECT

Abraham said, in effect, "I'm in the dark, I don't see things happening right now." So the Lord gave him this word of assurance, "As for you, you shall go to your fathers in peace; you shall be buried at a good old age" (Genesis 15:15). In short, he was told he would have a good life. And when you summarize Abraham's life at the end, he'd had it all. He had everything God promised to him—including another hundred years of life! At this time he was about seventy-five and thinking, "I'm getting old; I don't have much time left." But he would live to be one hundred seventy-five! He had more life ahead of him than he had behind him. The Lord was going to get it done; there was plenty of time to see God's promises fulfilled in his life.

> On the same day the LORD made a covenant with Abram, saying: "To your descendants I have given this land, from the river of Egypt to the great river, the river Euphrates." (15:18)

This is the first time the Lord had spelled out the dimensions of Abraham's inheritance. He had told him earlier, "Walk in the land through its length and its width, for I give it to you" (Genesis 13:17). Abraham had journeyed from Hebron to Bethel, down to Egypt, then back to Bethel. He was getting some idea of the "length and width," but I don't think he could have imagined *these* dimensions!

The Lord tells him, "Here are the dimensions of the land. And My dear son, it's bigger than you ever thought...and it's for you and your children after you."

David sang, "Lord, You have set my feet in a wide place" (Psalm 31:8). Oh, listen, child of God, the Lord wants us to learn personally that He will do larger things than we have ever dreamed possible. It may not come to pass in your or my preferred time frame, but let's be patient. Don't let yourself be squashed into a tiny, pigeon-holed way of thinking about the Lord's working toward you. God had said to Abraham, "I will...make your name great" (Genesis 12:2). Note those words carefully because He has great things in store for you too! Look for a moment at Paul's word to the Ephesians:

> I keep asking that the God of our Lord Jesus Christ, the glorious Father, may give you the Spirit of wisdom and revelation, so that you may know him better. I pray also that the eyes of your heart may be enlightened in order that you may know the hope to which he has called you, the riches of his glorious inheritance in the saints, and his incomparably great power for us who believe. That power is like the working of his mighty strength, which he exerted in Christ when he raised him from the dead and seated him at his right hand in the heavenly realms. (Ephesians 1:17–20, NIV)

We need to take a walk with God out under the stars. It's a *big* thing that God is doing with us, a great thing.

> "Eye has not seen, nor ear heard,
> Nor have entered into the heart of man
> The things which God has prepared
> for those who love Him."
> (1 Corinthians 2:9)

When Abraham gazed up at the stars that night, he couldn't discern the order in their pattern...he couldn't count their number...he couldn't understand their purpose...he couldn't see their beginning or end. He didn't know how this vast, powerful God was going to work all of these things out in his life.

He just believed Him.

Child of God, you and I were born for the stars, the skies, the heavens. We are heading toward something bigger than we ever imagined. Toward the end of Daniel's book, the prophet wrote:

> And many of those who sleep in the dust of the earth shall awake, some to everlasting life, some to shame and everlasting contempt. Those who are wise shall shine like the brightness of the firmament, and those who turn many to righteousness like the stars forever and ever. (Daniel 12:2–3)

How beautiful that is. The Lord says that we frail creatures of dust are headed for the stars. And the Lord's great and awesome plans include each one of us. Just remember that...when the will of God leads you into a season of darkness. The darker the night, the brighter the stars. His purpose for you reaches into eternity.

CHAPTER SIX

How to Deal with the Flesh

> Now Sarai, Abram's wife, had borne him no children. And she had an Egyptian maidservant whose name was Hagar. So Sarai said to Abram, "See now, the LORD has restrained me from bearing children. Please go in to my maid; perhaps I shall obtain children by her." And Abram heeded the voice of Sarai. (Genesis 16:1–2)

Sarah was still barren.

In spite of all the glorious assurances, promises, and divine visitations, nothing had really changed. Nothing at all. The days and weeks went by, and her infertility seemed to stretch out before her to the horizon like a gray, endless desert.

So, after ten years of waiting in Canaan, she suggested to Abraham a certain course of action: "Take my servant girl, sleep with her, and any children that result will be considered my children."

Sarah's "solution" wasn't some sexually promiscuous excursion on Abraham's part; it was a common domestic practice of that day. Jacob would later do the same thing. David, too, had several wives. While it was neither the Lord's original or ultimate design for marriage or for mankind's propagation, at that particular time in history this custom was not frowned upon by the

Lord. In the unfolding of redemption's vast recovery plan, God accepted with merciful tolerance the limited perspectives of a fallen race. And please note: Sarah's proposed plan was more for the provision of a *surrogate mother* than for her husband to take on a paramour.

To gain insight into this passage, we must first understand that what Abraham did wasn't wrong because of the *sexual* aspect of it. Where he and Sarah went wrong was in trying to achieve in the strength and energy of their flesh something which God had already promised. Rather than waiting for God to fulfill His word, they set out to "help Him" get it done.

That's the flesh for you! And when I speak of "the flesh," I'm referring to it

—as a designation for our human effort
—as a label for our flights of folly
—as it describes our limited view of God
—as that which brings blindness and unbelief
—as that which ever falls short of God's best, resulting in heartaches, confusion, and sin

And by the way, Abraham's excursion into "the flesh" doesn't leave you and me far behind! It's a sad fact of life that we tend to fall into the same fleshly patterns of life, characterized by impatience and carnal haste. And for all of us, the result is heartache and deeper frustration...as certainly proved true for Abraham and Sarah. The real problem is apparent at the end of verse 2: "And Abram heeded the voice of Sarai."

Now a woman who walks in the fullness of the Lord and His will has *everything* to contribute as a life partner. Solomon wrote, "A wife of noble character who can find? She is worth far more than rubies" (Proverbs 31:10, NIV). Yet in this case Sarah, with every good intention, brought the flesh center stage in their family—with its incalculable potential for harm and hurt.

Good intentions, it seems, don't necessarily produce good fruit in the will of God.

THE WAY OF THE FLESH

If you thumb back in your Bible a page or two to Genesis, chapter 15, verse 1, you will read, "After these things the word of the LORD came to Abram in a vision, saying, 'Do not be afraid, Abram. I am your shield, your exceedingly great reward.'" And the Lord said in verse 5, "Look now toward heaven, and count the stars.... So shall your descendants be."

God had spoken to Abraham in the clearest of terms with the firmest of promises. But Abraham *listened* to the voice of his wife. And while we may foolishly mock the intended beauty of marital partnership with cracks about whether or not it's God's will for a man to "listen to his wife," the real point stands: Abraham, the *husband,* was the failure. Not Sarah. Abraham listened to the way of the flesh and bought into the reasoning of the flesh. Sarah may have suggested something, but Abraham made the decision.

> Then Sarai, Abram's wife, took Hagar her maid, the Egyptian, and gave her to her husband Abram to be his wife, after Abram had dwelt ten years in the land of Canaan. (Genesis 16:3)

A significant amount of time had gone by. We shouldn't overlook the fact that there was some *reason* for Sarah to feel God needed a little help to get things moving. After so much time had passed, it's understandable why she might have reasoned, "Why are we just sitting around waiting to die? Maybe the Lord wants us to help ourselves a little bit here."

How often we allow ourselves to be confused in our understanding of God's timeless dealings with His children. Here's a truth you can take to the bank: *The Lord never violates His word.* He *always* does what He promises. When He says, "It will be this way..." it's going to be exactly as He said. Count on it.

Of course, we are always free to go stumbling along in the dark, saying,

"Well, let's see now...how was it supposed to be? Maybe what the Lord *really* meant to happen is this and that and the other..." But we won't remain in the will of God very long if we begin to explain away His words and rationalize our own impatience.

I can't help but think of our Simon Peter in this regard. Do you remember the situation in John 21? Jesus had recently been raised from the dead. Some of His disciples gathered beside the sea, waiting for His instructions, when Peter suddenly announced, "I am going fishing" (John 21:3). Several of Jesus' disciples apparently looked at one another, shrugged their shoulders, and said, "OK. We'll tag along."

The Bible doesn't provide an analysis of Peter's thinking in this passage, but it's easy to surmise what might have been going on here. When Jesus first called Peter, He told him, "Follow Me, and I will make you a fisher of *men*."

And it was true. They did catch men! Together, they "netted" lawyers and soldiers, prostitutes and Pharisees, tradesmen and tax collectors, rich and poor, men and women, boys and girls. It had been glorious! But now...well, where *was* He anyway? Yes, He was really alive, but was He truly going to meet them in Galilee as He had said? Peter had touched Him and talked with Him; Jesus was no ghost or mere vision. But what was going to happen next?

And even if Jesus was on His way to meet them, did Peter really want to face Him? Memories of his cowardly failure and denial burned in his gut like a fire. So what was he supposed to do? Just sit around on the beach feeling guilty? Patience had never been Peter's long suit!

When you read the account in John 21, it's very clear Peter wasn't going out on the boat just to clear his head or blow off a little steam. When he said, "I'm going fishing," he was talking about returning to his old vocation. I can almost hear the man saying to himself, "Well, I can't sit around forever. I'm going back to what I know. Sure, I know the Lord is real, and I've served my turn at His work, but fishing's work too, isn't it? And after all, even when He called me, Jesus said I would always be a fisherman (or something like that)!"

If we bandy words about long enough, we can end up justifying our fleshly alternatives to God's will. But, as with Peter, the Lord Jesus loves us too much to let us slide very far down that road. Look in John 21 and see how Jesus hooks the fisherman with a question, then slowly reels him in.

"Peter, do you love Me?"

"Yes, Lord."

"All right, then. Feed My sheep."

It's as though Jesus was saying, "Peter, you played around with that earlier metaphor I used—'fisherman.' Well work with this one awhile: I'm calling you a *shepherd.*" Suddenly there's no place of carnal retreat, no argument available, no opportunity to dabble with words. The Lord won't give any of us a place for the flesh, or for the flesh to analyze things to argue its own agenda.

In the same way, Abraham came to a point in life where he was completely bewildered by his circumstances. Abraham found himself saying, "I know the Lord said there's going to be children, but where are they?" He and Sarah must have thought, "Ten years have gone by and nothing has happened. Maybe we just don't understand how God meant to fulfill this promise." So together they weighed their options, took stock of their resources, and developed a plan to help the Lord work it all out.

In Genesis 16:4 we read, "So he went into Hagar, and she conceived. And when she saw that she had conceived, her mistress became despised in her eyes."

To a woman of that culture, childbearing was *everything*. It was evidence of her fruitfulness, her fulfillment, her favor with God, her very worth as a woman. So when Hagar realized she had conceived, she said—if not in so many words—"I'm better than you, Sarah." Now she was big potatoes—really big stuff! She was no longer just a handmaiden and a servant; she was a wife. And what was more, *she* would bear Abraham's first child! With every little word, every little gesture, and every little flutter of her eyelashes, she contrived to make her mistress feel like a second-class citizen.

Abraham's troubles had just begun.

WAYS THE FLESH ELBOWS IN

Listen, if you sow to the flesh, as Abraham did in this instance, there *will* be consequences:

> Do not be deceived, God is not mocked; for whatever a man sows, that he will also reap. For he who sows to his flesh will of the flesh reap corruption, but he who sows to the Spirit will of the Spirit reap everlasting life. (Galatians 6:7–8)

Hardly a week goes by without someone telling me he wants the Lord to deliver him from the results of his sowing to the flesh. While the person doesn't use these precise words, in essence he is saying to me, "I want to do exactly what I want—walking in disobedience and rebellion and sowing to my flesh as I desire—and then go running to the Lord and say, 'Lord, kill the crop!'"

People sow...but they don't want the harvest. They plant a field of thorny weeds and poison seeds and want the Lord to raise up strawberries and roses. Scripture says, "Don't be deceived on that score. It won't happen." Sowing to the flesh is a gravely serious matter. *If you sow to the flesh, there* will *be a harvest.* And the fact that you are a cleansed, forgiven son or daughter of God will not eliminate those consequences.

Abraham was called a friend of Almighty God Himself, the father of faith, and the patriarch of peoples and nations. But when he sowed to the flesh, he was not exempted. He, too, reaped the harvest.

Moses spoke with the Lord "face to face, as a man speaks to his friend," (Exodus 33:11), but when he indulged his anger, he reaped the harvest.

David was called "the man after God's own heart," but when he sinned, he reaped a terrible harvest with many tears and over many years.

Even before Ishmael was born, we are given an opportunity to see what Abraham's indulgence in the flesh will produce:

"He [Ishmael] shall be a wild man;
His hand shall be against every man,
And every man's hand against him.
And he shall dwell in the presence
of all his brethren."
(Genesis 16:12)

There would come a time when Abraham would see his son Ishmael on the verge of young manhood—at war with the world and wild as a desert wind—and Abraham would realize, "Dear Lord, have I got *problems.*"

And those problems are painfully present in the Middle East to this very day. Headlines shriek and cameras whir, relaying scenes of timeless conflict between the Arabs (descendants of Ishmael) and the Jews (descendants of Isaac). The hostility, feuding, and bloodshed dominate world concern and generate endless confusion—all because one man in a moment of weakness and impatience heeded the voice of the flesh. Scripture says Ishmael "shall dwell in the presence of his brethren." In other words, he's going to be right in the middle of things in that part of the world, with stress and trouble ever present.

That's a forecast about Ishmael, but it also illustrates what is true of the flesh. Give the flesh place in your life, and it will eventually run wild. We like to think we can control it, civilize it, sanitize it, and keep it under wraps, but we can't. Sooner or later, its place in our lives will be all too obvious. Sooner or later, "whatever you have said in the dark will be heard in the light, and what you have whispered behind closed doors will be shouted from the housetops for all to hear!" (Luke 12:3, NLT).

Incidentally, when we talk about the flesh, we are not talking about the devil. Jesus clearly taught that He is the deliverer from satanic bondage. Colossians, chapter 2, describes how Jesus, through His sacrifice on the Cross, made an open spectacle of the devil. The power of Satan and every demon of hell was *crushed* at Calvary. The grounds for our present overcoming as well as our ultimate victory over Satan and his demonic legions have been secured.

The flesh, however, is a different matter.

It can't be "cast out." We can't rid ourselves of its influence in some climactic encounter. What's more, the spirit of the world—our Adversary—while distinct *from* our flesh certainly plays *to* it as he manipulates every means possible in his ongoing quest to destroy us. But settle it in your mind: We will never be "delivered" from "the flesh" while we breathe on planet Earth!

But there *is* a way to deal with it! And we *can* win, if we will accept the terms of discipleship and Spirit-fullness. But the fact remains that you and I must *live* in and with our flesh—with all its attendant challenges, heartaches, and discouragement—for the remainder of our days.

However, there is great news of another fact: The day will come when there will be a glorious transformation:

> But let me tell you a wonderful secret God has revealed to us. Not all of us will die, but we will all be transformed. It will happen in a moment, in the blinking of an eye, when the last trumpet is blown. For when the trumpet sounds, the Christians who have died will be raised with transformed bodies. And then we who are living will be transformed so that we will never die. For our perishable earthly bodies must be transformed into heavenly bodies that will never die. (1 Corinthians 15:51–53, NLT)

Our human bodies with all their fleshly frailties and sinful inclinations will be exchanged for new and perfect spiritual bodies. And at *that* time our flesh and its power and quest for dominance in our lives will be slain and cast down forever.

In the meantime, however, let us keep this issue in balanced perspective. Yes, it's true that there are matters of bondage...handles in our nature which hell has gripped as we have ceded territory through ignorance, rebellion, and outright disobedience (Ephesians 4:27). And it is also true that once our flesh has surrendered that terrain to the devil, no amount of discipline can regain it. We need deliverance. At the same time, however, there are also matters of self-will and human indulgence from which a deliverance is not available. These selfish or carnal habits of conduct or attitudes of our old sin nature require plain, old-fashioned appropriation of Christ's life *for* and *in* us.

"Christ in you"—that sin-shattering power of His Cross and the death-breaking power of His resurrection—is our "hope of glory" (see Colossians 1:27; Romans 8:10–11). This is the gospel of victory over the flesh. But it isn't a "push-button liberation." Obviously, everybody would like solutions to their problems overnight. But hear me, loved one, you are *not* going to get a push-button liberation, any more than Abraham received a push-button appearance of the child of promise. He tried to work out the problem in the flesh, but he failed. But you can expect to find a victory over the struggles with "flesh" that we all have. The apostle Paul described the carnal battle which raged within himself in his letter to the Romans.

> I am carnal [i.e., "fleshly"], sold under sin [like a helpless slave]. For what I am doing, I do not understand [he's saying, "I can't figure out this puzzle"]. For what I will to do, that I do not practice; but what I hate, that I do [anyone here identify with this?]. If, then, I do what I will not to do,...it is no longer I who do it, but sin that dwells in me. [That's no excuse but an acknowledgment of a power that only Christ's power within can master.]
>
> For I know that in me (that is, in my flesh) nothing good dwells; for to will is present with me, but how to perform what is good I do not find. For the good that I will to do, I do not do; but the evil I will not to do, that I practice. (Romans 7:14–19)

All this drives the apostle to utter disgust with himself: "O wretched man that I am! Who will deliver me from this body of death?" (7:24). But just at this point of apparent futility, Paul turns to declare that certain victory is coming. Having confronted the "flesh"—detesting the self-centered, flesh-ruled life—he then answers his own question, "Who will deliver me?"

Here's the praise-filled key: "I thank God—through Jesus Christ our Lord!" (v. 25). Here is real victory over the flesh! Christ Himself, living within, will bring His person and power to bear on our weakness and proneness to sin by the in-working of the Holy Spirit.

This victory is for us, loved one. Once we come to that "wretched man that I am" point of being sick of our sin and the domination of our flesh, something can be done about it. But we need to *choose* to do it.

We may, in fact, choose not to. You or I can refuse this confrontation and appropriation; we can just go along, tiptoeing our way through the tulips of life, saying, "Well, I just wish, I *really* wish I could get the victory over that..." But there's something better: We can ask God's Spirit to overflow "Christ in us"...to bring us into victory over that sin area, boldly coming against the tantrums of the flesh. Scripture assures us that those who do this day by day will find a new power to "Walk in the Spirit, and you shall not fulfill the lust of the flesh" (Galatians 5:16).

But you and I must quit dabbling with the flesh! Because if we don't, there will be more "Ishmaels" born to us, and the harvest of pain may even outlast our own lifetime. Triumph over the flesh simply can't be worked out in our own energy or way, any more than it can be dispensed through an instant "deliverance" experience. There are certain areas of our self-life that need to be dealt with according to God's blueprint: the Cross and the Holy Spirit manifesting "Christ in you"!

HOW TO LIVE WITH THE FLESH

After she was mocked by Hagar, Sarah marched straight in to Abraham (I love this!) and said, *"My wrong be upon you!"* (Genesis 16:5).

I can just see Abraham sitting on his favorite cushion reading the evening paper when Sarah stormed in and threw that right in his face.

Strange as it may seem, she was right! It *was* Abraham's fault. The whole sorry scheme may have been her idea, but it was his responsibility. He didn't have to do what she suggested. She didn't impregnate Hagar; only Abraham could have done that.

> Then Sarai said to Abram, "My wrong be upon you! I gave my maid into your embrace; and when she saw that she had conceived, I became despised in her eyes. The LORD judge between you and me." So Abram said to Sarai, "Indeed your maid is in your hand; do to her as you please." And when Sarai dealt harshly with her, she fled from her presence. (16:5–6)

In a larger sense, Sarah was really saying, "Cast out the flesh!" So Abraham sent Hagar away. This, however, was not the Lord's way to solve the problem. We see in verse 9 that an angel went to Hagar, and "the Angel of the LORD said to her, 'Return to your mistress, and submit yourself under her hand.'"

Easier said than done! This would have been hard on Hagar, but at the Lord's direction, she returned to Abraham's household and submitted herself to her mistress.

As with Sarah, when *you* stand up and say, "Lord, I'm so tired of dealing with these fleshly habits; I want you to cast them out!" the Lord will—just as He did with Sarah in the return of Hagar—put the reality of the flesh right in your face. He'll say, "Look, you must live with it. You must live in a world of temptation and in a body riddled with sin's genetics...with inclinations and lusts of the flesh. But I'll show you how to overcome nonetheless, subduing the flesh through the power of *My* triumph—by the indwelling of My Spirit."

This is God's way. The flesh is to be dealt with on the basis of divine promises: "By which have been given to us exceedingly great and precious promises, that through these you may be partakers of the divine nature, having escaped the corruption that is in the world through lust" (2 Peter 1:4).

Though you and I will never in this lifetime be completely free from the downward tug of our flesh, God's Word of promise offers us a path of daily victory over every fleshly thought, every fleshly inclination, and every temptation to shortcut His timeline and "help Him out" through our own schemes. How? Well, here it is!

> There is therefore now no condemnation [no oppressive domination of sin] to those who are in Christ Jesus [for He is also *in them*!], who do not walk according to the flesh [by deferring indulgently to its whims], but according to the Spirit [through welcoming His ability to manifest Jesus' own character in us]. For the law of the Spirit of life in Christ Jesus [which, like the law of aerodynamics, can enable a plane to fly] has made me free from the law of sin and death [which, like the law of gravity pulls me toward a crash].... That...the law [of God's way and will] might be fulfilled in us who do not walk according to the flesh but according to the Spirit. For those who live according to the flesh set their minds on the things of the flesh, but those who live according to the Spirit, the things of the Spirit. (Romans 8:1–5)

The way the flesh is dealt with, then, is by reasserting the divine promises—employing the truth of the Word, the victory of the Cross, and the "promise power" of the Holy Spirit. The Word, the Cross, and the Spirit—the *triumph trio* for dealing with the flesh effectively.

Think of it! We have not only been called to *walk* in God's will, but we have been fully equipped to *live* in His will.

Hallelujah! What a Savior!

CHAPTER SEVEN

Responding to God's Presence

The Book of Exodus describes one of the most touching episodes in the life of any of the personalities of Scripture:

> So the LORD spoke to Moses face to face, as a man speaks to his friend. (Exodus 33:11)

How amazing that is! The mighty Creator and Sustainer of the universe talking to a man? Face to face? Friend to friend? It's an astonishing passage in the Bible, and it moves me deeply...but Moses wasn't the first to experience this wonder.

> Then the LORD appeared to [Abraham] by the terebinth trees of Mamre, as he was sitting in the tent door in the heat of the day. So he lifted his eyes and looked, and behold, three men were standing by him; and when he saw them, he ran from the tent door to meet them, and bowed himself to the ground, and said, "My Lord, if I have now found favor in Your sight, do not pass on by Your servant. Please let a little water be brought, and wash your feet, and rest yourselves under the tree. And I will bring a morsel of bread, that you may

> refresh your hearts. After that you may pass by, inasmuch as you have come to your servant."
>
> They said, "Do as you have said."
>
> So Abraham hurried into the tent to Sarah and said, "Quickly, make ready three measures of fine meal; knead it and make cakes." And Abraham ran to the herd, took a tender and good calf, gave it to a young man, and he hastened to prepare it. So he took butter and milk and the calf which he had prepared, and set it before them; and he stood by them under the tree as they ate. (Genesis 18:1–8)

How would *you* deal with encountering the presence of the living God?

THE LORD APPEARS IN HUMAN FORM

In Genesis 18:1 we read, simply, that "The LORD appeared to him [Abraham] by the terebinth trees of Mamre." Then immediately following we read that Abraham "bowed himself to the ground" before this Visitor.

But was this really *God Himself* who stood before Abraham?

We hear a lot of talk these days about angels and angelic visitations. Couldn't this have been an angel? Doesn't that seem a likely option? No, it is not a likely option when you consider that this Visitor allowed Abraham to bow down to the ground before Him. In short, He received Abraham's worship. If this had been merely an angel visiting Abraham, and not the Lord of heaven, the angel would have stopped Abraham quickly.

Angels are very sensitive about this issue! And understandably so. They have seen all too clearly what happened when one of their own number lusted after worship and exalted himself.

> "How you are fallen from heaven, O shining star, son of the morning! You have been thrown down to the earth, you who destroyed the

> nations of the world. For you said to yourself, 'I will ascend to heaven and set my throne above God's stars. I will preside on the mountain of the gods far away in the north. I will climb to the highest heavens and be like the Most High.'" (Isaiah 14:12–14, NLT)

Lucifer, "son of the morning," became Satan! No holy angel from heaven—no matter how powerful and exalted—would permit a man or woman to bow before him in worship.

The mighty angelic being described in Daniel chapter 10 was so awe inspiring and frightening that Daniel fell facedown to the earth before him. This may have been more sheer terror than worship! Even so, the angel made Daniel stand before he would speak to him:

> "Consider carefully the words I am about to speak to you, and stand up, for I have now been sent to you." (Daniel 10:11, NIV)

When the elderly apostle John had been shown all the terrors and wonders described in the Book of Revelation, he also was quickly and emphatically stopped on two different occasions—stunned with wonder—as he innocently tried to worship an angelic messenger.

> At this I fell at his feet to worship him. But he said to me, "Do not do it! I am a fellow servant with you and with your brothers who hold to the testimony of Jesus. Worship God!"
>
> I fell down to worship at the feet of the angel who had been showing them to me. But he said to me, "Do not do it! I am a fellow servant with you and with your brothers the prophets and of all who keep the words of this book. Worship God!" (Revelation 19:10; 22:8–9, NIV)

Every time in Scripture that a man started to worship an angel, the angel stopped him...*fast*. Unless, of course, we're talking about the "angel of light"—Satan. The devil will receive and delude people, hungrily accepting worship that rightfully belongs to the Lord.

But Abraham, who was living in the stream of God's will and responding to the promptings of God's Spirit, must have known this was no angel.

As the Lord came to Abraham on this occasion, Scripture records Abraham's response to the divine visitation in some detail. We see clearly how Abraham went about "waiting on the Lord."

This was a very *physical* appearance of God.

—Abraham fetched water to bathe flesh-and-blood feet.
—Abraham carefully prepared and served a meal—and God ate it!
—They visited together in the shade of a tree.

This incident has puzzled students of the Word for years. Some say, "I just don't understand how this could be! Was that really God?" Yes, this truly was a preincarnate, physical manifestation of the Lord God of Israel, sometimes referred to as "the Angel of the Lord."

And His name is *Jesus*.

The Son of God was manifest here, long before His incarnation, at which time Christ said, "A body You have prepared for Me" (Hebrews 10:5).

What, then, is the difference between this occasion—the Genesis 18 appearance of God—and the actual coming of Jesus in the flesh, born of a virgin? The great difference is that this time the Son of God did not come as *"begotten"* of humankind, nor did He come at this point to *dwell* among men. Christ didn't appear at Abraham's doorstep with the intention of living out life as a man—day in, day out, week in, week out. In the fullness of time, the Lord Jesus would experience the temptations, trials, and all the weaknesses that the flesh is subject to, and come through sinless and triumphant.

John 1:14 tells us, "And the Word became flesh and dwelt among us." The word *dwelt* literally means He pitched His tent among us; He came to be born, to live with us, to die, and to be raised again to life. But in the Genesis

18 visitation, that wasn't His goal. Here we are precisely told what He was doing: The Lord only *appeared* to Abraham.

He paid a call on him. He came to visit.

And Abraham said, "Please stay."

A SPECIAL APPEARANCE—BUT NOT UNIQUE

In Genesis 18 we are witnessing an early personal appearance of the living God. He has come to deal in an intimate, special way with people who are remarkably entwined with His covenant revelation to man. This is not the first time God has done this.

- He walked with Adam and Eve in the Garden in the cool of the day (Genesis 3:8).
- He wrestled all night with Jacob at the ford of the Jabbok (Genesis 32:22–32).
- He spoke with Moses, as we have mentioned, "face to face" (Exodus 33:11).
- He appeared in a dramatic way to Manoah and his wife before the birth of their son, Samson (Judges 13).
- He appeared to Joshua before the battle of Jericho as "Commander of the army of the Lord." Scripture underlines the fact that Joshua "fell on his face to the earth and worshiped" Him (Joshua 5:14).

The Man Joshua met outside Jericho was no less than the One who was Joshua's namesake, Jesus Christ. *Joshua* is the Hebrew word; the Greek word is *Jesus*. Joshua encountered face to face the One who was the fulfillment of everything that Joshua himself was just a *token* of. Joshua was leading the people to possess the land. He was the one who would show them how to be delivered from their enemies and how to possess what God had promised them. And later there would come a second "Joshua"—the One called *Jesus*—the One who would save His people from their sins. And just like His Old Testament namesake, the Lord Jesus comes to lead us in the conquest and possession of the things that are God's purpose for us too!

Loved one, do you believe that the same Lord who visited with Abraham, Moses, and Joshua wants personal companionship with you too? Could it be that in those moments of emptiness and loneliness in your soul, the living Redeemer is seeking to walk and talk with you?

WHEN THE GAUGE READS "EMPTY"

I recently felt a kind of "hollowness" in my soul. If I had been consciously compromising anything of a biblical life standard, I would surely have known it, as well as known that I needed to repent. But there was something else nagging at me, and I didn't have any definition for my feelings—only a sense of "empty."

One morning, not long after I had been alone at prayer—without much energy and with some latent frustration—I was passing through the kitchen on the way to my study. Anna looked at me, and her words confirmed my feeling: "Honey, do you think you need to go up to the conference a day early?"

Referring to my speaking engagement at a mountain retreat that weekend, she was suggesting that I make arrangements to arrive there early Thursday afternoon. I can hardly describe the "leap" within my spirit. She had not only sensed my need but had also recommended action. Though I had taken "days with the Lord" before, I had been too tied up in my frustration to think of the possibility of leaving early.

It would take paragraphs to describe what those few hours meant. As I drove through the mountains, I wept before the Lord with gratitude for His goodness and promises to me. I poured out my feelings of emptiness—my sense of "hunger"—and, as though it were the first time I had ever heard it, Matthew 5:6 was poured into my soul like liquid hope. I felt I was being filled with faith. I had confidence I was headed to a rendezvous with my Redeemer!

> Blessed are those who hunger and thirst for righteousness, for they shall be filled. (Matthew 5:6)

Suffice it to say, as I walked mountain paths, alone and in spoken communication with Jesus, *He visited me!* Words can hardly describe the exhilaration of being refreshed by "an overnight with Christ," but I still like to look back in my journal and be reminded of His faithfulness to refill, fully and readily.[1]

There is no place in God's Word that suggests we are to live on secondhand experiences with the Lord. I may be taught, cared for, and nourished by the help and counsel of pastors, spiritual leaders, and Christian friends. However, the One who saved me and called me to Himself also desires to draw me closer to Himself.

He is the One who knows when I sit and when I rise, who knows the thoughts and intents of my heart, who knows each word before it is spoken from my lips, who numbers the hairs on my head. Such biblical evidence of His personal attention indicates God is not merely taking statistical note of facts about my existence; it demonstrates God's desire to be personally attentive and involved with my life—*with me!*—in an ongoing way.

As the Lover of my soul and yours, He wants to be close, to disclose Himself to us, and yes, *to speak with us,* for our ears alone.[2]

RESPONDING TO HIS PRESENCE

The Lord had already appeared twice to Abraham. In Genesis 15, God established the covenant with him concerning the land of promise—Canaan. In

Genesis 17, the Lord appeared to him to establish the covenant concerning the birth of Isaac, Abraham's descendant. Now, in Genesis 18, the Lord appears again. But this time was different.

This time He had come simply to *be* with Abraham.

This is a lovely picture of how our dear Lord wants to come to abide with us, to walk with us in friendship. Christ said, "Abide in Me, and I in you.... I am the vine, you are the branches" (John 15:4–5). In other words, "Walk along with Me as you daily journey through your life. Stay close to Me, draw your very life and strength from Me, for without Me you can do nothing."

Abraham came face to face with his Lord, and his response to this encounter is a model of how the Bible would have "the seed of Abraham"—people of faith like you and me—respond to the presence of the living God.

Notice again these two verses:

> [Abraham] lifted his eyes and looked, and behold, three men were standing by him; and when he saw them, he ran from the tent door to meet them, and *bowed himself to the ground,* and said, "My Lord, if I have now found favor in Your sight, *do not pass on by Your servant."* (Genesis 18:2–3)

If I read this correctly, Abraham heard no one walk into his camp. There was no crunch of sandaled feet on the gravel, no whisper of clothing, no clearing of throats, and no murmur of voices. He didn't look across the shimmering heat waves in the distance and see them approach. He was sitting in the doorway of his tent, had looked down for a moment, and then when he looked up...they were just *there.*

Abraham had walked with God too many years not to recognize Him. This ninety-nine-year-old man leaped to his feet, *ran* to them, and prostrated himself on the ground in worship. The angels accompanying the Lord must have nodded with approval. Abraham's response was only right and proper. The Most High God had come to call at the home of a man!

Listen, friend, there is something powerful about the presence of the Lord coming to visit—whether it's in your heart, in your home and family, or in an assembly with other believers. Yes, in one sense He is always with us. He is everywhere present and never absent. But that was true in Abraham's day also; yet *this* order of visitation by the Lord holds a special quality.

There will be times like that in the life of every believer. Yes, the Lord is with us, and He has promised never to leave us or forsake us. Yes, His Holy Spirit indwells us and fills us. But there are wonderful moments or seasons in our walk of faith when—for whatever reason—His presence becomes very tangible and very precious. Suddenly you look up and *you know that He is there*. You sense His presence in the room. You catch the fragrance of His garments.

What do you do in those moments?

If you're not careful, you might miss them altogether! Listen, dear one, when the manifest presence of the Lord God moves among His people, *there is only one logical response*. The right response is to bow low before Him and say, "Lord, there is nothing better than this. This is *life*. Please don't go away. Please, please stay."

In the Book of Exodus, after the incident with the Golden Calf, the Lord warned Moses that He might remove His manifest presence from their midst and send an angel to guide them instead. Moses couldn't bear such a thought! In deep distress he said to the Lord,

> "See, You say to me, 'Bring up this people.' But You have not let me know whom You will send with me." (33:12)

And God replied to him:

> "My Presence will go with you, and I will give you rest." (33:14)

That was exactly what Moses wanted to hear. But to indicate the depth of his concern, he underlined the issue one more time:

> "If Your Presence does not go with us, do not bring us up from here." (33:15)

Those words simply well up inside me when I read them—and they have become the cry of my heart as well: *If Your Presence doesn't go with me, then God don't let me move!* I pray this about my own personal experience and my walk with God. I pray this about the life of the congregation I serve. It is a right and good thing to say to Him. *Lord, if Your presence does not go with me, don't allow me to go any farther. Lord, I don't want to walk without You. I don't want to serve without You. I don't want to close a business deal without You. I don't want to take one step without You.*

My mind moves to a pair of New Testament accounts. Late one night our Lord's disciples were out on the Sea of Galilee in deadly danger. A storm had swept across the lake, and they were straining with all their might at the oars, apparently getting nowhere. The Lord saw their plight and came to them, walking on the water through the darkness and the storm. They cried out in sheer terror, thinking (understandably!) that this must be a ghost—a demon from hell. On top of everything else they had to deal with that night, now they had to deal with spirits!

> Then He saw them straining at rowing, for the wind was against them. Now about the fourth watch of the night He came to them, walking on the sea, *and would have passed them by.* (Mark 6:48)

Jesus would have passed them by, but they called out in fear, and He answered, "Be of good cheer! It is I; do not be afraid" (Mark 6:50). Scripture says, "Then he climbed into the boat with them, and the wind died down" (v. 51, NIV).

Let's move ahead a bit in time to the days immediately following Jesus' crucifixion. The Bible says that on resurrection day, on the road to Emmaus, two of Jesus' followers were walking along, troubled in spirit by all that had taken place. A third party joined them as they walked. It was the risen Lord, but they didn't recognize Him. All along that road they poured out their hearts to Him, telling Him the tragedy of their Lord's death on the cross and the perplexing news that Jesus might be alive again.

As they approached the village that was their destination, we read in the Scriptures that the Lord "would have gone farther. But they constrained Him, saying, 'Abide with us'" (Luke 24:28–29).

The Lord is not in the business of fleeing from people, but hear me, please: *He is looking for people who will invite His presence and minister to His presence.* He is looking for people who will say, "Lord, don't go away. Don't walk on by. Don't move on down the road. Please abide with us!" Or, in the words of Abraham, "Do not pass on by Your servant" (Genesis 18:3).

You and I know very well that the Lord doesn't dwell in temples made with human hands, but somehow He does choose dwelling places where He can work among people. How does He choose these places? In some mysterious way I believe He is seeking men and women, boys and girls, who are longing after Him and saying to Him, "Lord, come *here*. Abide with us *here*. Why go elsewhere, Lord, when You are so deeply wanted and needed and loved right here and right now?"

There was a little song people used to sing a generation ago. It probably originated among believers somewhere down in the Caribbean. You may well have sung it at camp or around a campfire at some point in your life. "Kum by yah, my Lord, kum by yah." It means *"Lord, come by here."* Is that the cry of your spirit too? He's looking for people who will say, "Lord, we want You here. We want You to work here. We want to worship You here. We wait upon You."

Jacob, who had the Lord in a hammerlock in the middle of the night, said, *"I will not let You go unless You bless me!"* (Genesis 32:26).

Abraham said, "Don't pass me by" (Genesis 18:3).

Stay here, Lord. Please stay right here.

LEARNING TO WAIT UPON HIM

How do we do that? How exactly *do* we wait upon the Lord?

Let's trace the actions of Abraham for a moment. What did he do? He said, "Please let a little water be brought, and wash your feet, and rest yourselves under the tree. And I will bring a morsel of bread, that you may refresh your hearts. After that you may pass by" (18:4–5). Then he got his wife involved in the program:

> So Abraham hurried into the tent to Sarah and said, "Quickly, make ready three measures of fine meal; knead it and make cakes." And Abraham ran to the herd, took a tender and good calf.... So he took butter and milk and the calf which he had prepared, and set it before them. (18:6–8)

You see, here is a man who is literally *waiting on the Lord*. This isn't like waiting for a bus or waiting for a doctor appointment or waiting for Christmas. This concept of waiting becomes very clear when we visit a restaurant; how well we are *waited on* at our table determines in large part our response to the dining experience.

In the presence of the Lord, then, what should you do? How should you wait on Him? How should you serve Him?

"Well," you say, "I can't see myself running down to Ralph's Market and getting butter and milk and meat to serve to the Lord. Surely that's not what you mean, Jack."

Of course it isn't. But I do want to make it clear that just as surely as there were *physical* ramifications for Abraham's waiting on the Lord, so you and I have a *physical* aspect of waiting upon the Lord.

We are to wait on Him in humiliation at His feet

Abraham said, "Let me get a little water for Your feet" (18:4). The Lord is looking for people who will come humbly to His feet. That's where we should start! We come in submission, bowing down before Him at His feet. That's where the sinful woman came when Jesus was dining at the home of Simon the Pharisee.

> And behold, a woman in the city who was a sinner, when she knew that Jesus sat at the table in the Pharisee's house, brought an alabaster flask of fragrant oil, and stood at His feet behind Him weeping; and she began to wash His feet with her tears, and wiped them with the hair of her head; and she kissed His feet and anointed them with the fragrant oil. (Luke 7:37–38)

That's where Mary, the sister of Martha and Lazarus, came when Jesus dined in their home.

> Then Mary took a pound of very costly oil of spikenard, anointed the feet of Jesus, and wiped His feet with her hair. And the house was filled with the fragrance of the oil. (John 12:3)

Jesus treasured those moments! They were as choice and precious to Him as they were to the women who ministered to Him in that way. There is joy and healing and a deep sense of *rightness* to be found at the Savior's feet.

We are to wait on Him in worship

The Bible says that our worship before God is like sweet-smelling incense. In some unique way that we may never understand in this life, the mighty Lord of the universe seems blessed and moved by the praise and worship of His people.

In John 4:23, Jesus told the Samaritan woman, "The hour is coming and now is, when the true worshipers will worship the Father in spirit and truth; *for the Father is seeking such to worship Him.*"

The heart of worship is this: *My life needs God's presence to work God's purpose in my life.*

We are to wait on Him in sacrifice

When Abraham selected the calf, slaughtered it, and instructed Sarah to weigh out some meal, make bread, and then serve it all to the Lord, something very important was taking place: They were observing the rite of sacrifice. The meal and meat offerings they made to God were the forerunner of the worship that would characterize Israel's national worship in the future—the most important aspect of it being the slaying of animals for sacrifice. Abraham's words—"Make ready three measures of meal, and make those little cakes, and I'll go out and get a calf; we're going to wait on the Lord"—in a very real sense foretold how the Israelites would worship the Lord for centuries to come.

Those sacrifices and burnt offerings, of course, had much greater significance than the content of the offerings themselves. Many centuries later in Israel's history, the prophet Samuel would say to King Saul, "Has the LORD as great delight in burnt offerings and sacrifices, as in obeying the voice of the LORD? Behold, to obey is better than sacrifice, and to heed than the fat of rams" (1 Samuel 15:22).

King David would pick up this theme, too:

> You would not be pleased with sacrifices,
> or I would bring them.
> If I brought you a burnt offering, you would not accept it.
> The sacrifice you want is a broken spirit.
> A broken and repentant heart, O God,
> you will not despise.
>
> (Psalm 51:16–17, NLT)

To paraphrase, David was saying, "Lord, what we're doing here in Israel with all these sacrifices really isn't Your long-range target for us, is it? Your long-range plan isn't that we bring You meal offerings and meat offerings but that we come before You with open hearts, that we give You *ourselves*."

You and I don't sacrifice animals to the Lord anymore because the perfect sacrifice of God's Son has completely satisfied His righteous judgment against us—a judgment which we merited because we have walked in sin and disobedience. As believers, we have come to the living God and been justified through the blood of His Son Jesus Christ.

The sacrifice He wants now is YOU. *All* of you. Your total self on the altar. As Paul wrote: "I beseech you therefore, brethren, by the mercies of God, that you present your bodies a living sacrifice, holy, acceptable to God, which is your reasonable service" (Romans 12:1).

The Book of Hebrews adds: "Continually offer the sacrifice of praise to God, that is the fruit of our lips, giving thanks to His name" (13:15). So physical sacrifice—alive and aglow in the spirit—is the order of the day. *Every* day!

We are to wait on Him as willing witnesses

The prophet Isaiah saw the manifest presence of the Lord too:

> I saw the Lord sitting on a throne, high and lifted up, and the train of His robe filled the temple.... So I said: "Woe is me, for I am undone! Because I am a man of unclean lips, and I dwell in the midst of a people of unclean lips; for my eyes have seen the King, the LORD of hosts."
>
> Then one of the seraphim flew to me, having in his hand a live coal which he had taken with the tongs from the altar. And he touched my mouth with it, and said: "Behold, this has touched your lips; your iniquity is taken away, and your sin purged."
>
> Also I heard the voice of the Lord, saying: "Whom shall I send, and who will go for Us?" Then I said, "Here am I! Send me." (Isaiah 6:1, 5–8)

Isaiah was waiting on the Lord—before His very throne—and he heard Him say, "Now, who's going to go? Who's going to get about the business of waiting on the Lord, not only in worship but in their walk and witness? Where can we find a man or woman such as that?"

Isaiah said, "Lord, it sure couldn't be me! You know very well that I have stained and tarnished lips. I'm ashamed to open my mouth in Your presence. I'm unworthy to speak for You."

But then as the prophet waited before the Lord, an angel came with tongs and took a coal off the altar, and the very fire of God touched that man's lips, and the angel said, "Now your lips are purged." Isaiah's immediate response was, "Here am I. Send *me*. Let me have the privilege of ministering to You with my lips! Let me be Your witness!"

The Bible says that at Pentecost "there came a sound from heaven, as of a rushing mighty wind, and it filled the whole house where they were sitting. Then there appeared to them divided tongues, as of fire, and one sat upon each of them. And they were all filled with the Holy Spirit" (Acts 2:2–4). The Lord tells us that the indwelling presence of the Holy Spirit purges our lives with fire. And this brings about fresh praise and worship to the living God, who says, "Now those lips are qualified. Go into all the world and tell people. Let the message flow. Let the whole world know."

"LORD, HERE I AM!"

Abraham waited upon the Lord in a literal, physical way, and the Lord is looking for people who will wait on Him body and soul. He wants you to be a Christian of substance—flesh, bone, and blood—wholeheartedly devoted to Him. He desires your devotion where you work, where you walk, within your home. He wants you to praise Him. To wait on Him. To rise each day and stand with that physical body before the living God and say, "Lord, here am I. What will You have me to do this day? Do whatever you will with me. I am Yours!"

You may ask, "Where is the dividing line between ministry to the Lord and ministry to the world?" I don't think there is a dividing line! Jesus made the point very clear when He said:

> "The King will say to those on His right hand, 'Come, you blessed of My Father, inherit the kingdom prepared for you from the foundation of the world: for I was hungry and you gave Me food; I was thirsty and you gave Me drink; I was a stranger and you took Me in; I was naked and you clothed Me; I was sick and you visited Me; I was in prison and you came to Me.... Assuredly, I say to you, inasmuch as you did it to one of the least of these My brethren, you did it to Me.'" (Matthew 25:34–36, 40)

The point is, just get busy ministering in His name and in His power. But don't do it to be seen and appreciated by others; do it just for Him!

It all begins at His feet. It all begins in deep humility and recognition of our profound, bottomless, desperate, never-ending need of Him!

Linger before Him. And when You sense His very presence, just as close as He can be, invite Him to stay for a *long* time.

[1] The first six paragraphs of the section titled "When the gauge reads empty" are excerpted from pages 181–2 of the author's recent book, *Pastors of Promise,* © 1997 by Jack Hayford, published by Regal Books, and used by permission.

[2] The final three paragraphs of the section titled "When the gauge reads empty" are excerpted from the author's article "In Defense of Hearing God," published in the November/December 1996 issue of *Ministries Today* magazine, and are used by permission.

CHAPTER EIGHT

Faith Comes Out of Hiding

> Then they said to him, "Where is Sarah your wife?" So he said, "Here, in the tent." And He said, "I will certainly return to you according to the time of life, and behold, Sarah your wife shall have a son." (And Sarah was listening in the tent door which was behind him.) Now Abraham and Sarah were old, well advanced in age; and Sarah had passed the age of childbearing. Therefore Sarah laughed within herself, saying, "After I have grown old, shall I have pleasure, my lord being old also?"
>
> And the LORD said to Abraham, "Why did Sarah laugh, saying, 'Shall I surely bear a child, since I am old?' Is anything too hard for the LORD? At the appointed time I will return to you, according to the time of life, and Sarah shall have a son." But Sarah denied it, saying, "I did not laugh," for she was afraid. And He said, "No, but you did laugh!" (Genesis 18:9–15)

It was a hot afternoon, and Abraham sat in his tent door in the shade of the sheltering trees. As he looked up, he saw three men standing by him. But as we've noted, the visitors weren't men at all. It was the living God Himself, flanked by two powerful angels—all of them adapted to a human form for the purpose of this significant encounter.

God had come calling on Abraham, and the man from Ur had said, "Please stay with me for a while. Let me minister to Your needs." So it was that the Lord of all creation sat down in the shade with a human and shared a simple meal with him.

What an extraordinary encounter! Nothing exactly like it would occur again until the God-man Himself, the Lord Jesus Christ, would walk the dusty roads of Judea and Galilee with His followers, break bread with them, and share His very life.

Abraham was ninety-nine years old at the time of this visitation. Sarah was ninety. And God had come to say, "Abraham, I really meant it when I told you that you and Sarah would have a son. And now the time is almost here."

The Bible doesn't say this, but you can almost hear Abraham thinking, "Hey, if doesn't happen by the time I'm an even hundred, it probably won't happen!"

God promises Abraham that he and Sarah will have this son through the natural process. Sarah will become pregnant! They're not going to turn around in the tent one day and stumble over a baby that's been dropped out of the sky. She will go through what every expectant mother goes through; a baby will grow in her womb and emerge from her body as every other baby emerges.

Now Sarah was in the tent behind Abraham and his guests, listening to all of this. And since this was a tent and not a two-inch oak door, she didn't need her ear up to the keyhole. When that promise burst from the lips of the Lord, Sarah was scrunching herself as close as she could get to the front of the tent without making the fabric bulge. If she'd had a hearing aid, she would have had it turned up to ten. She didn't want to miss a word.

In the words of the King James Version, we read, "It ceased to be with Sarah after the manner of women" (v. 11). That's a nice, Old English way of saying she had passed menopause. At ninety, you would certainly think so!

The account adds, "Therefore Sarah laughed within herself" (v. 12). That laughter would become an issue in the conversation.

Another translation describes the incident like this:

> She laughed silently to herself. "How could a worn-out woman like me have a baby?" she thought. "And when my master—my husband—is also so old?" (v. 12, NLT)

"Worn-out" is a good rendering of the original language. She is saying, "My body is frayed and threadbare." She might just as easily have said the same thing about her faith. Not only was her body worn-out, but her hope had just about run the gamut.

Would she *really* experience such a pleasure? Would she *truly* experience the greatest aspiration and desire of her life—to hold a baby son in her arms? Within herself she's saying, "Could something so wonderful happen to a barren old has-been like me? A pregnancy? A baby? A son? At *my* age?"

In different circumstances you and I may have the same sort of reaction. We all have our own areas of barrenness. We have our own unfulfilled dreams and desires. And when we hear the Lord confirm His promise to us, we also long to take hold of that word and cling to it with all our hearts. Something within us begins to stir. Faith peeks through like a sudden shaft of sunlight on an overcast afternoon.

And yet, for all that (how often it's true)...we can't quite allow ourselves to believe.

Have you ever found yourself—in all candor—saying, "Lord, there are those places in my life where I just don't see anything happening. There's no change. No movement. No fruit. No breakthroughs. And, well...it just seems like I've waited a long time!"

"A long time" is relative, isn't it? Abraham and Sarah had been waiting a quarter century since God had first promised them a son. And Sarah, if she wedded at age fifteen or so, which was common in that culture, could have been waiting for a good *seventy-five years*.

Now that's a long time. But for some of us, if a week goes by without visible results, it's "a long time." You long for something to happen, and after six or seven days slip past, you begin to despair. After a month, it's almost hopeless. And after three months? Well, forget it. It's futile. Might as well give up.

Sarah had said, "I'm worn out. My body is shot, and my heart isn't far behind." *But then...who* was *that on the other side of that tent fabric? That was no ordinary visitor. And—what was He saying? A baby? Could it really be?*

Behind what she thought was the privacy of her tent, Sarah was completely silent in her thoughts. She said nothing. She uttered no sound. She was probably even holding her breath. But when she heard the promise—the very thing she longed for with all her heart—she laughed within herself. And the Lord God, who monitors our every thought, heard that silent laugh and knew it for what it was.

In a future day David would marvel over God's ability to "hear" our thoughts. He wrote, "You know my every thought when far away.... You know what I am going to say even before I say it" (Psalm 139:2, 4, NLT).

In this account, Scripture says:

> And the LORD said to Abraham, "Why did Sarah laugh, saying 'Shall I surely bear a child, since I am old?' Is anything too hard for the LORD?" (Genesis 18:13–14)

Just who is that person hiding behind the tent door, afraid to be totally exposed to the possibility of a miracle?

To tell you the truth, she looks a lot like me. And maybe she looks like you too.

SHRINKING BACK FROM A MIRACLE

The reason you and I tend to shrink back from the possibility of a miracle is not because we don't *want* a miracle. In fact, we couldn't want anything more! Sarah had yearned for a son for years. And standing right outside the tent door was the living God of the universe who had condescended to manifest Himself in the midst of her household situation and say, "What your heart has hungered for, My daughter, is about to happen. The waiting is almost over. Fulfillment is just around the corner."

Upon hearing that, Sarah laughed within herself, and there's something so plaintive and poignant about that laugh. It bears a little scrutiny. Eventually that miracle baby, who would be born in less than a year's time, would be named for what had occurred in that moment: His name would be Isaac, or "Laughter."

Have you ever been praying or reading the Scriptures and heard the Spirit of God whisper something like this: *My son, My daughter, the time is right. This is for you*? Sure you have. And when that promise comes to your heart, what happens? Sometimes hope suddenly wells up within you, and you find yourself thinking, "Oh, could it be? Could it be? *Wouldn't it be wonderful?*"

I believe those very thoughts were in the heart of Sarah on that hot afternoon in the tent. I believe that she trembled on the very threshold of belief and that within her laugh was a flash of hope, wanting to express itself. The words she had heard were so sweet, so tantalizing, so exciting that—in spite of herself—her heart began to pound and her hope began to soar within her. But then that old self-protection instinct sprang up, like a fire-prevention sprinkler system ignited by a little match. And instead of a joyous, full-throated laugh of belief, it became a cynical, fearful chuckle. What began as a flicker of hope ended with a quenching fizzle of cynicism and doubt.

And at some point in life that has happened to each person reading this book. It may have happened to you even today. During the course of the things that transpired today, there perhaps has begun to rise in your heart the hope, the expectancy, that God is about to fulfill a long-standing promise to you in an extraordinary way. Better than anyone else, you know those places of barrenness and fear and doubt in your life. For years and years, you've clung to the Lord's promise that He is about to do something in that very area of your soul. But nothing has happened yet. And then the Lord speaks again very clearly, and hope springs up in your life like a fragile daisy poking up through the gravel.

Sarah had lived twenty-five years with a promise. And with each passing day its fulfillment seemed less and less likely. Then one afternoon in the heat of the day, the Lord came calling, and the word came again, "You shall *certainly,* certainly… It *shall* be!"

"Oh!" she must have said with a laugh. "*Oh*…oh, but that's silly, isn't it? For a moment there, I nearly believed it."

You may at this moment be within an inch of opening your heart to a miracle of God:

- You know that you have never received the love of God and you need to open your heart to Him as Savior and Lord. The time has come. He's calling you! Something rises up from deep down inside of you that says, "Oh, yes, that would be peace, that would be love." *But you're afraid to take that step.*
- You know that you have never allowed yourself to be filled and empowered by God's Spirit, as Scripture commands. Something within you yearns for that touch on your life and wants to reach out in belief. *But your heart has been barren for so long! Do you dare to believe?*
- You know that God wants to set you apart for some special ministry or service to His people. You hunger for Him to use you in that way. You long to be His instrument to touch and bless other lives. You've become convinced that it's His desire too. *But how could He use some-*

one with your background, with your finances, with your limitations?

- You've been almost afraid to pray for a friend or loved one who is hostile to the faith. He's been so hard, so closed. She's been so cynical and so self-sufficient. But the Lord is encouraging you to step out now and specifically ask for that man's or woman's salvation. You want to believe He *could* do it. You want to believe He *would* do it. *But him? But her? It seems so wildly improbable.*
- You're in a church that hasn't shown any spiritual fire for years. You long for God to move in a fresh way within the body. You want to see old feuds set aside. You want to see that sleepy apathy swept away in a fresh outpouring of the Spirit's working. Somehow you know that God wants that, too, and you feel a little kindling of hope. *But how could it happen? It's been dry and dead around here for years and years!*

You sense the Spirit of God saying to your heart, "I will fulfill in you everything I've promised to you. And you need not fear rejoicing in it." The laughter starts to bubble up...then hope dies, and the laughter becomes sad and hopeless on your lips. "Aw, why am I getting excited? Life's just going to go on the way it's always been."

The Lord said to Abraham, "Why did Sarah laugh? Is anything too hard for Me?" Great question! And you could state it in one of several ways:

—*Is* anything too hard for the Lord?
—Is *anything* too hard for the Lord?
—Is anything *too hard* for the Lord?
—Is anything too hard for *the Lord?*

Would you care to answer that question? Do you—from your heart—believe His Word that "No good thing will He withhold from those who walk uprightly" (Psalm 84:11)? Do you—from your innermost being—believe His Word that "the LORD will perfect that which concerns me" (Psalm 138:8)?

Why are we so reluctant to tell Him our heart's desires? Are we afraid that He might not touch that area of our lives because it's "too hard" for Him? Or because He's just unwilling to bless us? I recently spent a week with about seventy pastors, many of them with small, struggling congregations. One day I said to the group, "Why don't we just go ahead and say, 'Lord, You know what's best, but I would like more people to minister to'?" It was an uncomfortable concept for some of them; they couldn't bring themselves to do it. Now, in no way did I want to minimize the importance of small ministries in needy, out-of-the-way places, but some of those men had labored so long and had been so frustrated, wanting with all their hearts to touch a community for Christ. Some of them were a little like Sarah on that hot afternoon—tired in body, tired in faith, and a little bit afraid even to hope.

Like many of us, some of those pastors didn't want to "come out from behind the tent door" and open themselves up to the possibility of a miracle. They didn't want to say out loud what was really eating at their hearts because... Because why? Because they were afraid the Lord couldn't do it? Because they were afraid the Lord didn't want to do it? Because they were afraid He might not really care about the deepest longings of their hearts? They had forgotten the prayer of Jabez, where a young man with the nickname of "Pain" boldly asked the Lord to expand his borders—to roll back the boundaries of his influence. And Scripture says, "God granted him what he requested" (1 Chronicles 4:9–10).

How many of us are hiding behind a tent door, unwilling to step out into the open and say, "Lord, I thank You that I am going to receive what You have promised"?

FULL-TERM PROMISES

Scripture says, "At the time appointed I will return to you, according to the time of life, and Sarah shall have a son" (Genesis 18:14). That's another way of saying, "This is going to be a full-term baby."

That means a little bit more waiting, doesn't it? And that's not the answer we're looking for! We don't want nine months of carrying a child...nine months of bearing a promise until it comes to the moment of delivery. We want to wake up in the tent one morning and have a crib in the corner with a baby crying in it. For that matter, we'd prefer that the baby be smiling and cooing. Or maybe standing up and walking and talking with a full vocabulary.

We don't want to wait! We want roses, but we don't want to weed or prune or water or wait until they bloom in all their fullness. Nor do we want to acknowledge that God might be maturing those roses—and bringing fragrance into our lives—through some dark, rainy, overcast days.

I can remember when people had to wait for their radios or televisions to warm up before they could see or hear anything. No one thought much about it at the time. But can you imagine anyone putting up with such a thing now? I can remember when people had to dial a number with a rotary dial. What a Stone Age concept! We need one-button, preprogrammed auto-dial. Speed! No waiting! Immediate fulfillment! We can't have last year's computer because it takes "too long"—maybe three or four seconds—to perform functions that used to take hours. We are all schooled to instant gratification. We pray, "Lord, give me patience—and I want it *right now!*"

Yet the Lord said to that dear elderly couple, "At the time appointed I will return to you, according to the time of life." My wife, Anna, had to carry two of our children during the heat of the summer months, and these were no light-weight infants. One of them weighed in at ten pounds, eleven ounces. My wife has had over forty pounds of babies (as I sometimes put it); that's four children averaging over ten pounds each! I've watched her go through some seasons with real difficulty. The waiting becomes long! Nine months can seem like nine years, and I can imagine ninety-year-old Sarah saying, "Lord, You promised us a child twenty-five years ago. Now, couldn't you just send him by the stork or Federal Express? Do we have to wait *again?*"

But the Lord had said, "at the appointed time." This was going to be a regular baby on a regular schedule born in the regular way.

And there is an "appointed time" for you, my friend. He will be faithful to His word, and He will respond to the heart's desire of His children. What He delivers may not be the very thing you asked for, but it will be the very thing you need. He will bring fruitfulness to that place where emptiness has reigned, and He will cause your desert to blossom like a rose.

It may not take twenty-five years, but however long it takes, it will be worth the waiting. In fact, while you go through the test of waiting, you will learn more about the Lord's miracle-working grace in your life than you would have learned if you had received a next-day delivery.

The Lord said to Abraham and Sarah, "The miracle for which you have waited will come. But it will be something that grows in your life and comes forth in the fullness of time."

THE FINAL STEP

As we continue reading the text, Sarah apparently emerges from the tent. In my imagination I can almost see this dear lady finally daring to slip through the front flap and step out into the visible presence of the Lord. That's when the Lord said, "Why did Sarah laugh?" Can't you just imagine the fear that gripped her heart at those words?

> But Sarah denied it, saying, "I did not laugh," for she was afraid. And He said, "No, but you did laugh!" (Genesis 18:15)

I like this added touch to the story. It reveals someone taking the last step when faith comes out of hiding. It takes place when we hear the Lord say to our hearts, "You're afraid, aren't you?" and we honestly reply, "Yes, I am." When we 'fess up to our fears in this way, a beautiful thing occurs. We discover that God's grace is greater than our fears, that fear doesn't disqualify us from receiving His promises. We hear God reply, "Your fear doesn't make any difference in My care for you or My promise to you. In spite of fears, I'm going to get this job done." And His love begins to cast out the last fear.

> And the LORD visited Sarah as He had said, and the LORD did for Sarah as He had spoken. For Sarah conceived and bore Abraham a son in his old age, at the set time of which God had spoken to him. And Abraham called the name of his son who was born to him—whom Sarah bore to him—Isaac. (Genesis 21:1–3)

It was Laughter! Isaac! He fulfilled the promise, right there in her arms! And with that rose a joy...bringing the laughter of the spirit that has learned the sufficiency of God's grace and power overcoming our fears and our hiding. It comes from the deep places of our being...full-hearted laughter, uncolored by any doubt, unshadowed by any fear. It resounds like an echo through the canyons of our past wanderings in wonder—"Will God ever...?" And the answer is a joy-filled yes! He will *always* remember the promise and never neglect our longings.

Step out.

Don't be afraid to welcome the prospect of such laughter as Sarah's.

CHAPTER NINE

The Power of Total Commitment

If You, LORD, should mark iniquities,
O Lord, who could stand?
But there is forgiveness with You,
That You may be feared.
(Psalm 130:3–4)

And Abraham journeyed from there to the South, and dwelt between Kadesh and Shur, and stayed in Gerar. Now Abraham said of Sarah his wife, "She is my sister."

And Abimelech king of Gerar sent and took Sarah. But God came to Abimelech in a dream by night, and said to him, "Indeed you are a dead man because of the woman whom you have taken, for she is a man's wife."

But Abimelech had not come near her; and he said, "Lord, will You slay a righteous nation also? Did he not say to me, 'She is my sister'? And she, even she herself said, 'He is my brother.' In the integrity of my heart and innocence of my hands I have done this."

And God said to him in a dream, "Yes, I know that you did this in the integrity of your heart. For I also withheld you from sinning

> against Me; therefore I did not let you touch her. Now therefore, restore the man's wife; for he is a prophet, and he will pray for you and you shall live. But if you do not restore her, know that you shall surely die, you and all who are yours."
>
> So Abimelech rose early in the morning, called all his servants, and told all these things in their hearing; and the men were very much afraid. And Abimelech called Abraham and said to him, "What have you done to us? How have I offended you, that you have brought on me and on my kingdom a great sin? You have done deeds to me that ought not to be done." Then Abimelech said to Abraham, "What did you have in view, that you have done this thing?"
>
> And Abraham said, "Because I thought, surely the fear of God is not in this place; and they will kill me on account of my wife." (Genesis 20:1–11)

Abraham's experience of God's grace, patience, and amazing kindness finds its parallel in our lives. We've all experienced that divine tenderness as we fumble and bumble our way along, seeking to walk in His will. He moves in our lives to redeem us, make the crooked places straight, and save us from the worst of ourselves.

But here is something that continues to amaze me.

Even after you and I have experienced one revelation after another of God's glory and grace—as Abraham had—it's astounding how easily we can turn right around and fall into an old, all-too-familiar trap of the flesh...as though we had never experienced the touch of God on our lives at all.

Now, the Lord had appeared to Abraham. As we have already seen, he had stood where few in the history of the human race have ever stood: face to face with the almighty God! And standing there before "the Judge of all the earth," he had entered into a bold intercessory ministry, pleading first for a decadent civilization and—failing that—for the rescue of his nephew's household from a fiery judgment.

But even after all the growth and victories and profound spiritual experiences in Abraham's life to this point, Genesis 20 looks for all the world like a tiresome rerun of the earlier episode in Genesis 12: *Abraham's misadventures in Egypt.* It's the same bad song, and the second verse is even worse than the first! Abraham falls back into the same deception and cowardice that dogged the earlier part of his walk with God.

We could say, "Shame on you, Abraham."

We could say, "How *could* you, Abraham?"

We could shake our heads and cluck our tongues at him.

We could do those things, except...except that so many of us are prone to do the very same thing!

Few of us have room to judge. Every one of us needs recurrent visitations of God's grace and patience as we follow on—often stumbling. No matter how long we walk the pathway of His will, there will always be precarious footing and potential pitfalls...until we plant our first step on the Other Side.

AN OLD STUMBLING STONE

Let's set a target. Let's get a handle on truth that can help us avoid some of the dangers of this pathway, strewn as it is with stumbling stones. Review with me the words which open this chapter, as Abimelech asked Abraham, "Why did you do this to us?"

It's a fair question. Why did Abraham lie and deceive people who had never harmed him, bringing them into the danger of God's judgment? It just doesn't figure! God had said to Abraham that through him all the nations of the earth would be blessed. But this certainly wasn't a very auspicious start.

"I did it," Abraham answered the king, "because I thought the fear of God isn't in this place," which, being translated, means: *"I was afraid for my life!"*

Bottom line, it's a pretty chicken-hearted explanation. Too bad Abraham didn't have a wise Promise Keeper buddy to take him to breakfast for bagels and eggs. His iron-sharpening-iron teammate might have said to him, "C'mon, Abe! Square with the truth—you need to face your fear. Admit it, you're trying to save your own hide!" With that sort of partnership and fellowship (and how we all need it!), Abraham might have been spared this digression into folly.

As it turned out, however, Abraham became a case study of an important spiritual principle: Before we may enjoy the fulfillment of God's highest promise to us or through us, *we will have to learn to quit shielding ourselves, seeking to save face or trying to save our lives.*

If we pause for a moment to bow and listen carefully, we can hear the echo of a voice Abraham had not known in his time. It is declaring to us—and to all who would know the fullness of God's will—that "whoever desires to save his life will lose it, but whoever loses his life for My sake will find it" (Matthew 16:25).

As Abraham devised a plan to shelter himself from the possibility of his demise (at the expense of Sarah), something happened to him that also happens to you and me at times. Abraham projected his own fear upon others.

"They're not afraid of God," he claimed. "They're going to take my life." What he was saying of course is "I'm afraid of *them.*" This fear for physical safety overwhelmed both his reverential fear of God and his fear of violating trust with his wife. Abraham's blindness to the power of his misplaced fears became the bondage from which he needed release.

Even later, when his deception was revealed, Abraham wasn't exactly quick to own up to his error. Instead, he temporized..."But indeed she *is* truly my sister. She is the daughter of my father, but not the daughter of my mother; and she became my wife" (Genesis 20:12). Anyone recognize himself or herself here? Amazing, isn't it, how effective our courtroom skills become when we are rationalizing our own righteousness! So Abraham attempted to lead the justifiably skeptical Abimelech through the twisted path of his own logic and to construct a rationale for the messy situation he had created. As for Abimelech, he just wanted to get the incident closed—in a hurry!

> Then Abimelech took sheep, oxen, and male and female servants, and gave them to Abraham; and he restored Sarah his wife to him. And Abimelech said, "See, my land is before you; dwell where it pleases you." Then to Sarah he said, "Behold, I have given your brother a thousand pieces of silver; indeed this vindicates you before all who are with you and before everybody." Thus she was rebuked. (vv. 14–16)

Here is a remarkable example of grace…an abundance of mercy in the face of abysmal failure. Thank God, "where sin abounds, grace does much more abound" applies for us all. Note carefully what happened next.

> So Abraham prayed to God; and God healed Abimelech, his wife, and his female servants. Then they bore children; for the LORD had closed up all the wombs of the house of Abimelech because of Sarah, Abraham's wife. (vv. 17–18)

Here was Abraham, a man burdened with his sense of recent failure, a man just victimized by his fears, *now* moving into a stance of ministry. It's a further expression of how completely the Father commits to fulfill His promises and purposes in us. His man Abraham had been appointed to be a man through whom blessings would abound. As Abraham interceded on behalf of Abimelech and his household, God's mightiness was manifest, notwithstanding Abraham's weakness.

The Lord turned this situation around in a big way…just as He is so willing and ready to do for us.

As we ponder this awesome demonstration of God's ability to rescue His own from their foolishness and weakness, several extremely important life principles emerge. These are lessons that will assist our own pursuit of God's will and bring us further along the road in His ways.

Principle 1: Yesterday's revelation of God's wisdom doesn't preempt the potential of today's folly

You and I need to walk with a holy caution. We all need to carefully guard the terrain where our spiritual victories have been won. Though we may have experienced manifestations of God's glory and power toward us in the past, we must never suppose we can't be victimized by our own flesh all over again! There is nothing that delights our Adversary more than tripping us up *in the very areas where God has previously granted us victory!* Satan longs for revenge and lurks in the wings, strategizing his retaliatory strike.

We are always in great danger if we think we can rest on our laurels or suppose we've moved beyond the carnal knee-jerk tendencies of our past. One victory in the battle doesn't signal the end of the war. It just means it's time to reload!

I can't help but think of Samson in this regard—one of Israel's most renown judges, a man who had accepted the oath of a Nazirite. A Nazirite was a person who had agreed to separate himself from others for a given length of time by consecrating his life to God with a special vow (see Numbers 6). The Nazirite oath included not touching any dead thing, not drinking any alcoholic beverage, and not cutting their hair.

Now the Lord had told Samson's parents that he was to be a Nazirite *from birth,* set apart as a very special vessel for God's use. He had been *raised* with these values; it was not a come-lately requirement trumped up in a moment of excitement. Samson knew the rules, so the speak, and he was not ignorant of the fact that his effectiveness in fulfilling his call and maintaining his power was linked to those vows.

We usually focus on Samson's infamous haircut as the act that brought down this powerful man. But even before that pivotal event, another aspect of the Nazirite vow had already been violated.

Do you recall when Samson was going down to the Philistine villages and was suddenly attacked by a lion? The episode is recorded in Judges 14:6, where God's Word reports how the Spirit of the Lord came upon Samson. Supercharged by God's power, he caught hold of the lion by its jaws and literally *tore the creature in half.* It was a moment of high triumph, and young Samson walked away from that encounter a victor, tasting for perhaps the first time in his life the power and splendor of God's Spirit in his life. But there's more, sad to say, on the flip side of that record.

Some time later Samson returned to the scene of his great victory where the carcass of the lion was still lying. Now Samson knew very well that the Nazirite vow, which had shaped and guided his life from earliest memory, specifically forbade him to touch any dead thing. But Samson noticed a bee hive in the open cavity of the carcass. And just as he would later demonstrate an apparent lack of sexual discipline in his life, at this point Samson chose to indulge his yearning for a bit of forbidden sweetness. He stooped over the animal carcass and scooped out some honey, probably supposing his snack was inconsequential—especially since no one was there to witness his compromise.

That "honey out of the eater" would later become the enigma in a riddle he would use to confound and mock the Philistines. But the puzzling thing wasn't how this mighty man could spin a play on words out of a beehive in a dead lion. The truly baffling thing was how a man whose life had been so consecrated to God and so filled to overflowing with the power of God's Spirit could so casually disregard his vow to the Lord!

The Bible says a three-fold cord is not *easily* broken, but it doesn't say it *can't* be. The three-fold vow of Samson's Nazirite commitment—the secret to the will of God for his life—began to unravel right there. He deliberately touched a dead thing, and thus *at the very scene of a great victory brought about by the power of the Spirit of God,* he opened the door to defeat!

While there are important differences in the stories, you might notice a similarity in Samson's situation and Abraham's. Abraham had stood face to face with the Lord only days, or at most a few weeks, earlier. He had seen the astonishing victory of the Lord—an angelic deliverance of Lot and his family from the destruction that rained down on Sodom and Gomorrah. Yet he turned right around and fell into a ridiculous snare that had earlier tripped him. Recovering from that earlier fall, he had come back to the Lord and rededicated himself to following God's will (Genesis 13:1, 4).

But then he stumbled again. Over the same lousy rock in the road.

Please listen, dear one. If you have experienced a victory in your life through our Lord Jesus Christ, you're called to *stand* in that victory (Galatians 5:1)! You and I are solemnly warned never to relax our vigilance and never to return to a dangerous confidence in the flesh!

But if we do, I want us to see something of God's glorious grace in this Old Testament picture of the Spirit of God leading a person forward in the Father's will. Even though Abraham stumbled from a great height, at the bottom of the pit the Lord picked him up and started him out on the path of His purpose.

Again.

Principle 2: The fear in our hearts doesn't have to stop the flow of our lives

Yes, Abraham fell back into the same absurd, fleshly snare the Lord had rescued him from earlier in Egypt. But despite this, please read 20:1: "Abraham journeyed from there to the South."

Abraham was still in motion. There's something to be said for that.

When you read the words "Abraham journeyed from there," remember that he was journeying from the place where he met God and two holy angels face to face. His movement forward indicates a measure of wisdom that deserves affirmation. Abraham resisted the inclination to respond as Peter would two thousand years later.

Do you remember the incident on the mountain? There in that lofty place with Jesus, James, and John, Peter saw the transcendent radiance of the transfigured Christ. Stunned by the visitation of divine glory, Peter proposed establishing a shrine and remaining there permanently. "Hey," he said in effect, "this is glory land! This is where things happen! I'll just pitch my tent right here and settle down."

Peter's remarks reflect that old human tendency to enshrine our experience and remove the responsibility for further growth. In Abraham we see a man who recognized the *ongoing* purposes of God, as He would lead us from place to place, from experience to experience, and from battle to battle. Abraham realized that God is not bound to any one experience or geographic location. He understood that to pursue the will of God is to remain available to move ahead.

Change—even change in the will of God—can be very difficult for some of us to handle. I've even heard of churches splitting over the fact that the leadership remodeled the worship center and removed the old pews. "But I got *saved* sitting in that pew!" some will protest. "We sang hymns to God's glory in those pews. You take out those pews, and *God's* going to leave this place!" But God does not restrict Himself to physical places or physical objects or to our private experiences or doctrinaire biases. We all need to be *shapable,* available to God's ongoing transformation of our heart and mind and life. Change is necessary if we're committed to pursuing God's will for our lives. Remember this: It isn't static!

So Abraham was in motion—he was moving along in trust. He was not looking for security at the carnal level our humanness tends to seek. And in heading south, Abraham was risking the insecurity of the unknown. He was heading out—the same man who many years earlier left behind the comforts and security of Ur and then later exited Haran to follow God's leading. Yet in strange contrast to those bold steps of faith, in Genesis 20:2 we see him fall lamely back on the fleshly arm of support.

How in the world do we reconcile this? How do we account for it?

To be honest, I don't know how to account for it...but I'm afraid I've sometimes become a pretty fair illustration of it! How about you? On some occasions we can believe God so *easily,* but at other times we find our flesh fighting furiously to maintain its foothold. We are reminded (again) that growth in the Lord involves a *daily* dying to self (Luke 9:23). Sometimes hourly!

Facing the subject of dying to ourselves in a spiritual sense, we naturally react as we would if our physical lives were threatened: "Oh, don't take my life!" Why? Because what becomes true in the *spiritual* "me" inevitably *becomes* the physical "me"—that is, it impacts the real day-to-day world I live in. When we are called to lay down "our lives," we each face different issues. It can be any of the thousand and one things the flesh prizes beyond the ultimate fulfillment of God's purpose in our lives.

I remember so well God's call to the pastorate of the church I now serve. It was a time in my ministry when wonderful doors of opportunity seemed to be swinging open before me on every hand. After fifteen years of service and labor, I was at the point of reaping the rewards: a well-established, prestigious pastorate in a major city with a secure salary. The breaks were there—at last! Yet at the same time God was saying, "Will you follow Me *here?*" I knew very well where He was pointing, and I wanted no part of it! It was a tiny congregation with a little building in an obscure community, offering a barely adequate salary. All things considered, it seemed to offer a future of permanent obscurity.

Those weeks in my life, though now distant in time, are as real in my memory as yesterday morning. "My son," the Father was saying to me, "will you give Me your *life?*" He needed to bring me to the place where I didn't give three hoots about whether or not I remained an obscure person for the rest of my life. When that issue was settled—after weeks of internal warfare—God was liberated from that point on to do what He wanted to do with my life.

He asks the same of all of us. Regardless of our vocation or surroundings, God's purpose and will challenges us at an elemental level in our lives.

It will confront our fear of *being thought less of*...
It will call us beyond our *dependence on things*...
It will command our willingness to *believe beyond what we can see.*

Just recently somebody was talking to me about one of the great public ministries of this generation, a ministry known throughout the world. It is led by a pastor-teacher who preaches to multiplied thousands of people each week. The man I was speaking with made a comment about this leader. He said, "I believe that if you were to take that pastor and tell him that next week he would have just twenty people to preach to rather than the thousands he preaches to now, he would say, 'So be it. It's the Lord's ministry. I'm not afraid.'"

I agree. Not only because I know the man but because I know just a little about the *plan*—God's plan! When He has *us*, then He is free to open up reservoirs of blessing and grace beyond anything we've ever experienced. Freedom from a fear of God's will—especially the *dying* it entails—works the release of everything.

When your life isn't your own anymore, when you give it up and say, "Do what You will with me, Lord," the doors of possibility will open. The Lord wants to rid us of our fearful desire to protect ourselves, that sense of self-preservation that lurks in our hearts. Gracious Redeemer that He is, He waits patiently while we deal with those fleshly fears of loss and uncertainty.

My own struggle with God's call to accept an obscure pastorate lasted for six weeks. For others, that struggle may go on for years, as the flesh screams for survival. Yet where there is a heart that truly longs for His will, the Father remains patient. As David wrote, "He understands how weak we are; he knows we are only dust" (Psalm 103:14, NLT). Even while we're clutching and clawing, and the flesh is maneuvering, the Lord will not give up on the heart that's set on pursuing His will.

Principle 3: The overruling providence of God is exercised for those who are committed to God's will

One of the grandest things I've ever learned about the will of God is wrapped up in one sentence. Hear it, dear one: *If you're surrendered to the will of God, you can't miss it!* The God who knows our hearts is faithful to transcend our weaknesses if—*if*—the heart is wholly His. True, Abraham had some weak self-preservation still lurking within, but it is inescapably evident that Abraham's heart belonged to God. He had said on an earlier occasion, "I have raised my hand to the LORD, God Most High, the Possessor of heaven and earth" (Genesis 14:22). That was more than a ritual expression or a formal gesture. In uttering those words, he was saying, "My heart is in God's hands. I'm given over to Him."

OK. Fine, Abraham...but what about those fears of yours?

"Oh, man, why'd you have to bring *that* up?"

Yet right on the heels of Abraham's surrender to those fears, we encounter two of the loveliest, most powerful words in all of Scripture:

> *"But God..."* (Genesis 20:3).

There have been books and songs, poems and sonnets written about those two words. How often do we fumble along and louse things up, and just as everything appears hopeless, *"But God..."* The Lord rescues us. Hallelujah! There is salvation in those words. There is hope and healing and grace in those words.

"But God" is a theme that runs from one end of Scripture to the other. Man does this, man does that, man gets in so far over his head he doesn't have a chance of recovery...*but God...!*

> "But as for you, you meant evil against me; *but God* meant it for good...to save many people alive." (Genesis 50:20)

> David stayed in strongholds in the wilderness.... Saul sought him every day, *but God* did not deliver him into his hand. (1 Samuel 23:14)

> My flesh and my heart fail; *but God* is the strength of my heart and my portion forever. (Psalm 73:26)

> "You killed the author of life, *but God* raised him from the dead." (Acts 3:15, NIV)

> Eye has not seen, nor ear heard, nor have entered into the heart of man the things which God has prepared for those who love Him. *But God* has revealed them to us through His Spirit. (1 Corinthians 2:9–10)

There is yet another "but God," and on this instance, our eternal destiny hangs in the balance! Read these next words very carefully.

> And you He made alive, who were dead in trespasses and sins, in which you once walked according to the course of this world, according to the prince of the power of the air, the spirit who now works in the sons of disobedience, among whom also we all once conducted ourselves in the lusts of our flesh, fulfilling the desires of the flesh and of the mind, and were by nature children of wrath, just as the others. *But God,* who is rich in mercy, because of His great love with which He loved us, even when we were dead in trespasses, made us alive together with Christ (by grace you have been saved), and raised us up together, and made us sit together in the heavenly places in Christ Jesus. (Ephesians 2:1–6)

The words "But God..." are the mammoth pivot of our personal histories.

"I was doing this, *but God...*" "I was going there, *but God...*" "I was headed hellbent in this direction, *but God...*" Abraham was moving on in faith, yet the shadow of fear gripped his heart, and he gave in to cowardly deception.

But God started working anyway!

The Lord confronted a pagan king in the middle of the night and said, "Stop what you're doing. Stop it right now, or you're a dead man."

It's a curious fact, but in order to help us do the right thing, the Lord may sometimes get the attention of an unbeliever sooner than He can get *our* attention! I remember an occasion some time ago when a non-Christian approached me, wagged a finger in my face, and made that all-too-familiar accusation, "And you call yourself a *Christian?*"

In our flesh we want to rise up and defend ourselves. But sometimes the wisest course may be to simply bow before the Lord and say, "Lord, I receive that rebuke." The Lord may work through unbelievers in this way to jar us into examining our hearts. Some might counter, "Well, I've heard people say things like that, and they were just spitting out hatred." Maybe so, but receive the rebuke anyway! You don't need to receive the hate, just receive the correction.

You may be tempted to say in your defense, "But I really wasn't doing that much. He misunderstood me. She misread me." Don't defend yourself! Let the Lord be your defender. If you try to justify yourself, protect yourself, and save your own life, you may wade into the same sort of mess that Abraham did. But God in His overruling providence overshadowed Abraham's cowardice and failure and told Abimelech, "You get things straightened out with this man. Give him back his wife."

Abimelech did what he was told. And in the process the Lord spared Sarah the violation of her purity and spared Abraham from harm as well.

I have to chuckle when I read in verses 7–8 of Genesis 20, "But if you do not restore her, know that you shall surely die, you and all who are yours. *So Abimelech rose early in the morning.*"

I should think so! He was up with the chickens *that* day! I don't know how early he rolled out of the sheets, but the Bible says it was early. As never before in his life, this pagan king was motivated to cooperate with the will of God. And that's yet another encouraging thought: In His irresistible sovereignty, God can even turn our most feared opposition into the very solution to our dilemma.

Principle 4: The redeeming grace of God will transform the fruit of our fears into a harvest of faith

In verse 6, God said to Abimelech in a dream, "Yes, I know that you did this in the integrity of your heart. For I also withheld you from sinning against Me."

How many times I've heard people say, "You know, I just really feel the Lord wants me to do thus and so [you fill in the blank], but I'm afraid I might do the wrong thing." Listen, God put the brakes on a pagan king who was bent on the fulfillment of his own lust and who had taken a woman, thinking she was available to him (at least he apparently had some scruples). If God would stop *him*, where there was not even a covenant relationship, then count on it, friend, when you or I—as *redeemed* children of God's covenant—honestly deal out of the integrity of our hearts, the Lord is certainly not going to let us wander too far afield. Let me illustrate.

Some time ago, the Lord dealt with me about giving a sizable offering to a particular Christian ministry. Then later, on two separate occasions, He stirred me again, urging me to give the *same* amount of money to that *same* group. The third time the Lord spoke to me on this matter, I thought to myself, "Hey, wait just a minute. I'm in a rut. I've got this thing in my mind about that particular ministry. Maybe it isn't of the Lord after all. Maybe it's just been *my* idea all along." Deep down, however, I realized I didn't really want to give that amount of money. It wasn't that I had anything against the ministry, but if I was going to give that much money, I would have preferred to put it into a few favorite ministries at my own church. (That's not being selfish, I told myself.)

I can still see myself walking down the hallway of our home and into the bedroom, contesting: "Lord, am I supposed to give this money? I just don't know whether You've told me to do this or whether this is originating in my own mind."

The answer was immediate and clear: "Son, if you thought it was Me and it wasn't, and you gave out of the integrity of your heart, do you believe I would let you be hurt in any way?" Instantly the issue was settled. I obeyed, giving exactly as I had felt I was to do.

Child of God, let me urge you to respond to the impulses of the Holy Spirit on your life without fear. Some say, "I'm so afraid of getting out of the will of God. I just don't want to take the chance of operating in the flesh." God doesn't want you to do that either. So when you believe you are moving forward in His will, say to Him, "Lord, I submit this situation (this decision, this conversation, this action) to You, and I trust You to stop me in my tracks if I'm making a mistake. The door seems to be open to me right now; but Lord, You know I want Your will more than anything else. Please close the door in a hurry if this isn't right, and I will trust You!"

Contrast that with the approach taken by people who say, "God told me to do this and I'm gonna do it, come hell or high water. I don't care what anybody says to me!" That attitude is simply wrong. The Spirit-led believer would say, "Lord, I believe You've shown me something I should do in Your will, and I will just do it out of the integrity of my own heart." If you do this and there is something God wants to stop you from doing, He'll stop you. It's that simple. He'll get you out of a mistake you make out of ignorance.

Now, if you do the wrong thing out of *disobedience,* erring willfully, then you've got another kind of problem on your hands. In that case you will suffer the consequences of your sin. But if you or I innocently transgress the perfect will of God while pursuing it in the integrity of our heart—praise God!—He'll be there to protect, defend, and resolve issues by His grace and providence.

What was it Solomon said?

> Trust in the LORD with all your heart; do not depend on your own understanding. Seek his will in all you do, and he will direct your paths. (Proverbs 3:5–6, NLT)

Just look at Abraham! He made a terrible blunder, but God was sovereignly watching over his life, leading him back to the straight path. After a royal foul-up, the next thing we know he's in the king's palace laying hands on the royal family and ministering to them in the authority of the Lord!

MAKE A FULL-HEART SURRENDER TO THE PURPOSE OF GOD

Let's glance ahead a moment to Genesis 21.

> And the LORD visited Sarah as He had said, and the LORD did for Sarah as He had spoken. For Sarah conceived, and bare Abraham a son in his old age, at the set time of which God had spoken to him. And Abraham called the name of his son who was born unto him—whom Sarah bore to him—Isaac. (vv. 1–3)

In verse 2 we see that expression "the set time." Do you know what just explodes in my mind as I read this passage of Scripture? Even Abraham's slowness to respond to God's word with full faith did not alter God's fulfillment of His promise to Abraham and Sarah *at exactly the time He said He would do it*. Why? The answer, I believe, is in the title of this chapter: "The Power of Total Commitment."

Abraham's heart of hearts was fully committed to the way of the Lord, and on the basis of that wholehearted commitment, God's wholehearted care and attention assured the perfecting of His purpose in Abraham.

So, my dear brother or sister in Jesus, if you have not yet made a complete abandonment of yourself to the purpose of God in your life, let me encourage you to do so. You can spend a lifetime trying, hoping, struggling, and straining, and never realize anything approximating the high fulfillment and fruitfulness awaiting you in our dear Lord's purpose for you. But He *will* reveal His purpose to anyone who will say, "Lord, I lift my hands to You. I give everything I have and everything I am over to You."

This full-heart surrender does not preclude the very real possibility that we may continue at times to struggle with weaknesses in our lives. A secret corner of fear. A recurring shadow of doubt. An unhealthy craving of the flesh. Listen, those things are present in every one of us—even in the most dedicated and the most surrendered of us. And there will be those times when the flesh raises its head and whispers, "Protect yourself...spare yourself...save yourself." But—hear me again!—*but* if there has been that prior commitment, a total commitment to His will and purpose, God will remember and honor that commitment. He'll do whatever it takes. If God has to move on a pagan king in the middle of the night to get the situation straightened out, He will. And what's more, He can turn the situation into a *ministry opportunity*, as His redemptive grace is expressed through you.

AND BEYOND THOSE FEARS

Loved one, the God who knew you prior to your birth and summoned you to His Son also knew very well the weaknesses of the flesh with which you would struggle—as He knows mine. And He is committed to bringing us along in this winding pathway toward our ultimate release and full realization of His will.

"But, Jack, there are those embarrassing weaknesses," you persist.

Yes. And that's precisely the point of this chapter: to see that in spite of our weaknesses, the Lord works in and through these lives of ours, and He gets the job done *right on time*.

How often do we groan inside and say, "Oh, if I had only known that sooner!" But the fact is, we *didn't* realize it sooner. We learned it as we moved along the pathway in the will of God. Abraham could have learned some things sooner, too, in his pilgrimage. But he didn't. Even so, my friend, *Isaac was born anyway*.

That promised child arrived right on schedule. And in the same way, the *image of Jesus Christ* will arrive in you and me; *the purpose of God* in each one of us will be manifest. Once a total commitment is in place, even though total *perfection* is greatly lacking, leave the sanctifying and perfecting of your life up to Him. Moment by moment. Day by day. Through all your years.

He'll get the job done, all right. And He'll get it done right on schedule.

CHAPTER TEN

The Ultimate in God's Will

Now it came to pass after these things that God tested Abraham, and said to him, "Abraham!" And he said, "Here I am." And He said, "Take now your son, your only son Isaac, whom you love, and go to the land of Moriah, and offer him there as a burnt offering on one of the mountains of which I shall tell you."

So Abraham rose early in the morning and saddled his donkey, and took two of his young men with him, and Isaac his son; and he split the wood for the burnt offering, and arose and went to the place of which God had told him. Then on the third day Abraham lifted his eyes and saw the place afar off. And Abraham said to his young men, "Stay here with the donkey; the lad and I will go yonder and worship, and we will come back to you." So Abraham took the wood of the burnt offering and laid it on Isaac his son; and he took the fire in his hand, and a knife, and the two of them went together. But Isaac spoke to Abraham his father and said, "My father!" And he said, "Here I am, my son." Then he said, "Look, the fire and the wood, but where is the lamb for a burnt offering?" And Abraham said, "My son, God will provide for Himself the lamb for a burnt offering." So the two of them went together.

> Then they came to the place of which God had told him. And Abraham built an altar there and placed the wood in order; and he bound Isaac his son and laid him on the altar, upon the wood. And Abraham stretched out his hand and took the knife to slay his son. But the Angel of the LORD called to him from heaven and said, "Abraham, Abraham!" And he said, "Here I am." And He said, "Do not lay your hand on the lad, or do anything to him; for now I know that you fear God, since you have not withheld your son, your only son, from Me." Then Abraham lifted his eyes and looked, and there behind him was a ram caught in a thicket by its horns. So Abraham went and took the ram, and offered it up for a burnt offering instead of his son. And Abraham called the name of the place, The-LORD-Will-Provide; as it is said to this day, "In the Mount of the LORD it shall be provided."
>
> Then the Angel of the LORD called to Abraham a second time out of heaven, and said: "By Myself I have sworn, says the LORD, because you have done this thing, and have not withheld your son, your only son, in blessing I will bless you, and in multiplying I will multiply your descendants as the stars of the heaven and as the sand which is on the seashore; and your descendants shall possess the gate of their enemies. In your seed all the nations of the earth shall be blessed, because you have obeyed My voice." So Abraham returned to his young men, and they rose and went together to Beersheba; and Abraham dwelt at Beersheba. (Genesis 22:1–19)

In a life of towering peaks and deep valleys, this was the highest peak and deepest valley of all.

As it happened, the crowning moment of Abraham's life didn't occur in the course of the Lord's three dramatic appearances to him. Nor did it come with the birth of Isaac, the miracle baby and the fulfillment of God's long-standing promise. No, the crown of Abraham's life occurred on a barren mountaintop, the very same mountain, some believe, where two thousand years later the Son of God would be crucified for the sins of the world.

Abraham was asked to do precisely the same thing that the almighty God of the universe would do two millennia later: He was asked to sacrifice his only son on that mountain,

> *the son who was the fulfillment of all his expectations;*
> *the son who was the beating heart of all his hopes and dreams;*
> *the son who stood at the very center of God's covenant and promise.*

What happened on that lonely mountain in a land called Moriah would for all time picture the greatest sacrifice of all.

WALKING WITH ABRAHAM

Abraham was a pioneer of faith in God. As we have seen, he spent most of his life seeking to possess a promised land—a land he never did fully possess himself. He also spent much of his life despairing over the absence of a promised son who wasn't born until Abraham was pushing the century mark. But despite all the uncertainty and disappointment in his life, Abraham was committed to pursuing the will of God.

When you and I roll out of our beds each morning, we're on the same terrain—setting out to walk stride by stride with Abraham. As with him, we go out not knowing what a day holds. As with him, we are dead and barren in ourselves, as inadequate to bring living promise into this world as Abraham and Sarah were. Until the Lord ignites the power in the promise, we sense little prospect of becoming a people from whom life flows. But the Holy Spirit has a way of bringing us *on the way* along the path of the Father's will. He reveals how the reigning power of Jesus Christ *in* us can produce His fruitfulness *through* us.

Jesus *is* the resurrection and the life; as He lives within us, His life flows through us. Where our hands reach, His will touches, and *healing* occurs. Where our lips speak, His voice sounds the living Word of God and begets life—creative and delivering in its power.

Most of us would love to find a shortcut to the power and intimacy of Abraham's walk with the Almighty. We would prefer that it just drop down upon us as a shining mantle of glory from heaven. We long for miracles of God's grace and power to drip like diamonds from our fingertips wherever we go. We want the fragrance of heaven to permeate our garments and follow us into every situation.

Well and good. Ah, but there is a *process* in our development. There is a price tag that comes with our refinement. We've seen it happening in Abraham, as the Lord tested, tried, purified, and perfected this man until He accomplished the purpose of God in his life.

So it is as we meet Abraham at this culminating point of his life. It would still be many years before his death. As a matter of fact, Abraham wouldn't die until he was 175 years old. He would outlive Sarah by many years, remarry, and father several more children. But at this lonely pinnacle of his earthly pilgrimage, God's ultimate goal for Abraham's life was realized.

And that ultimate goal, my friend, is not that we might arrive at some place where we walk on water or have miracles flow through our fingertips. No, His goal is that we come to the place in our walk with Him where we so grasp His nature and His ways that we are ready to abandon ourselves to His direction, to move in response to any call and to *trust Him completely*.

The desire of God's heart is to bring us to the place where we will never again doubt His character and His nature. This is the place in life where God's Word becomes so absolutely secured in our heart that we will walk forward in empty blackness—even when there seems no immediate divine presence or momentary direction for our steps. It is a place where we come to *know* God's Word will never fail us, nor will His presence ever leave us.

In this thin slice of Abraham's history, the patriarch prepared himself to climb a mountain. He couldn't have known it at the time, but he would be leading his son to the same place where the living God would one day lead *His* only Son—the delight of His heart. Abraham's obedience at this dramatic moment would become a timeless portrayal of God's plan of redemption. When Abraham led Isaac up that mountain, he became an instrument in the hands of the Almighty to reveal the very picture of what God Himself intended to do—to work redemptively, to deliver marvelously! But it never would have taken place if Abraham had not come to the place where he believed God's nature and presence so completely that he followed on in God's *will* even when he didn't understand God's *way.*

This, I believe, is the objective of the Lord's working in all of our lives. *His purpose is to develop within us a total receptivity toward doing His will, a total abandonment to His ways, a total readiness to do whatever His Word and His wisdom direct us to do.* He is drawing us toward a steadfast solidity of trust, to a walk with Him that evidences our conviction that He will never violate Himself or His Word. He will do for us all that He has promised, no matter the circumstance or our questions of the moment.

ANCHORS IN A TURBULENT WORLD

You and I are not called to be a people gathering in small holy huddles, clutching our righteous garments to ourselves and hoping we can preserve ourselves until Jesus comes. We are not called to clasp hands in safe, sanctified circles, wistfully whispering "Maranatha" to one another in hopes the Lord will beam us up out of this present darkness. Rather, Jesus is looking for a people who will begin to *penetrate the darkness* by the flow of His life in and through them. He seeks to bring us to the place in our pilgrimage where we'll stand firm and trust Him even when it grows so dark we can't see or understand what's happening. He wants to hear us say from the heart, "He is *my* faithful Lord, and He will not change."

There is a desperate need for anchors in this society of shifting walls and crumbling foundations, for people who have an unshakable grasp on the Rock that is Jesus Christ and who evidence a resulting solidity and confidence wherever they are and with whatever life delivers to their doorsteps. That quality of grounding comes from the very sort of life experiences through which the Lord brought Abraham.

You and I don't covet these sorts of stretching, sometimes heartrending experiences, do we?

Perhaps one of the reasons we don't is that we misunderstand what it really means to know God's will. Ultimately, God's will is not scrutinizing and analyzing a long list of daily life details. What does the Lord want me to do today? Who does He want me to talk to? Where does He want me to go? etc., etc.

Pursuing the will of God ultimately means *pursuing God Himself*. It means learning His ways and walking in obedience to the limit of our understanding.

And beyond.

FAITH IN MOTION

I had a pleasant conversation with one of the young men of our church recently. As we talked, I encouraged him not to remain stationary any longer, waiting for the Lord's specific, step-by-step direction, but to begin to *move*. I wasn't suggesting he jump into something without prayer or pondering or counsel, but I wanted him to understand that God directs those who are in motion, trusting Him for guidance. I suggested that he set out on a wise, well-considered course, believing God to direct him as he went along. Solomon said much the same thing when he wrote,

> A man's heart plans his way,
> But the LORD directs his steps.
> (Proverbs 16:9)

If you want to know the Lord's will, don't just stand out in the middle of a wheat field and wait for a stone tablet to drop out of heaven with the words "Go to Thailand" or "Enroll in Bible college" or "Enlist in the marines" or "Study medicine" or "Marry Sam" inscribed on it! That isn't the way the Lord does business with us. He calls us to follow—to begin trusting Him *on the way* in our lives. He says, "Come, child of God, and let Me direct your steps!"

His movement is never a desperate, frenetic rush to bring change into your life. You won't hear God gasping, "I've got to do something quick!" So if you find yourself saying, "I'm not sure where I'm going, but I'm going to get there fast!" just cool your heels. Faith is neither sweaty, desperate, nor panicked. It's really more a matter of saying, "Lord, I sense You have a purpose You want to work out in me, so I'm moving forward as Your peace abides with me."

The Word says: "Let the peace of God rule in your hearts" (Colossians 3:15). As you put one foot in front of another, keep saying in your heart, "Lord, if You want me to go in a different direction than the one I'm pursuing, well, I'm not in a hurry. I'm simply proceeding as best I understand." Then trust the Holy Spirit to make the way you go fruitful, *or* to change your direction, or reorder your way. Simply remain wide open to those possibilities in your heart. But don't fear *movement* simply because you don't have a specific direction for every issue or step or decision in your life.

LEARNING THE LORD'S WAYS

You and I tend to worry so much about the little details of our three-score-and-ten that we sometimes miss the *larger* purposes of the Lord. Listen, the principal matter of knowing God's will doesn't involve knowing all the myriad minutia about His way *today,* so much as it means beginning to understand His ways *for all time.*

In Psalm 103, David makes a striking statement about the Lord:

> He made known His ways to Moses,
> His acts to the children of Israel.
>
> (v. 7)

You can find any number of people who want to see the Lord's actions. They want to see Him *doing* things. Of course, that isn't bad in itself. I'm one of those people! I love to see the Lord working wonders. I delight to see Him moving in power, moving in my life, moving in our church, moving in a thousand and one daily situations. I love to see the Lord's acts. But I'm concerned about something even more significant than that as a preparation in my own heart.

I need to understand His *ways*.

When our greatest longing is to understand the Lord's ways, it will eliminate the necessity of our having to see something happening all the time to be sure He is there. More and more the heart learns to understand that what God is doing may not be easily observed. People who have to see the sunrise to be sure another day is coming are people who will live in fear of the dark forever. But people who know that God has ordered the course of this world—and that the sun *is* going to come up—don't worry about the darkness of the night. They are secure in their confidence that another day will dawn.

Learning the Lord's ways is more important than seeing His acts. God showed His *ways* to Moses, but the crowd saw His *acts*. The crowd got excited about the smoke and the fire and the earthquakes and the miracles, but Moses knew Him as a Friend. Listen, dear one, don't permit yourself to run around from church to church, meeting to meeting, ministry to ministry, event to event, looking for the latest, most dazzling, great happening of God. The ultimate desire of the Lord is finding people—and He found one in Abraham—who simply do whatever God says to do, right where they are. He's looking for people who say, "I am settled. I know the ways of my God. I may not understand what's going on around me right now, but

I know

that I know

that I know

He does not change!"

THE TEST

Now it came to pass after these things that God tested Abraham. (Genesis 22:1)

Every phrase in this verse is important.

After these things. After what things? After Abraham had followed God for half of his hundred years—pursuing the way of the Lord, learning lesson after lesson, fumbling, failing, triumphing, and finally seeing the fulfillment of promise. After all *these* things over a period of fifty to sixty years, God brought this man to a time of testing.

Most of us would like the fulfillment and results of what happened with Abraham and Isaac without any of these things spoken of in verse 1. Nor do we want the test of verse 1. But it just doesn't happen that way. We can't have the gold in our lives without allowing God to sift us through tests and refine us through fire.

[God] said to him, "Abraham!" And he said, "Here I am." (v. 1)

How I love that reply! Abraham was saying, "I'm here, Lord. I'm ready, Lord. I'm listening, Lord, for whatever You might say to me. Here I am." Why so willing? Because Abraham recognized the voice. He knew very well Who was speaking to him.

But the *words* that familiar voice spoke next—they just didn't compute.

> "Take now your son, your only son Isaac, whom you love, and go to the land of Moriah, and offer him there as a burnt offering on one of the mountains of which I shall tell you." (v. 2)

It staggers the mind. It doubtless stunned Abraham—stopped in his tracks by an apparent reversal in the character of the living God. *Sacrifice a child?*

This command of the Lord must have shaken the old man to his bones. This shockingly specific directive gave every appearance that the God he knew and followed had somehow changed His very nature! God's command to sacrifice Isaac ran counter to everything Abraham had learned of *this* God. The Lord—Yahweh—was different from the gods of the nations.

Human sacrifice was never a part of the worship of the Most High. The satanic worship of ancient Babylon, near where Ur lay, and the Canaanite worship of Baal and Ashteroth surrounding him certainly demanded human sacrifices. These demon-gods lusted after blood! For this very reason, God would later tell Israel to march in and completely eradicate this culture.

Yet in spite of the wild currents of thought that must have coursed through his brain all night long, Abraham rose up early in the morning and started the journey. It overwhelms me to think about it! He simply got up, woke up his boy, loaded his mules, and began that nightmare journey. If it had been me, I think that would have been a day when I could have found a great many things to do around the house. "Right, I'll do what You say, Lord, but You know, I just remembered that I've got a fence out there in the back forty that needs repair. Wouldn't be right to leave Sarah and the hired servants with that job. Lord, how about a week to enjoy Isaac before we climb that mountain?"

How would *you* have responded? The Bible tells us that Abraham rose up early in the morning and headed out.

> Then on the third day Abraham lifted his eyes and saw the place afar off. (v. 4)

As I read this sentence, I can't help but think of a grieving father's heart. I believe there is more taking place here than a man traveling along a dusty road in the wilderness! In the Bible's description of Abraham's lifting his eyes and looking ahead, I see more than a man peering off into the distance to see what lay on the horizon. Here is more than a man lifting a moistened finger to the wind to determine which way it's blowing.

When the Bible says he lifted his head, I think it's reasonable to assume Abraham has been walking with his head down, perhaps for a long time. Pondering. Searching his heart. Racking his weary mind. "What is God doing? Why me? Why now? Why this?" Yet please note: He neither stopped nor delayed. He continued the journey. He kept putting one foot in front of the other, though his thoughts were locked in a puzzle.

Listen, loved one. There will be times when you are puzzled by the Lord and wonder what's happening to you. Consider Abraham! Let this man's pathway of pursuing God's will help you keep moving in the direction He has shown you—even through your tears. Yes, there may be times when we, like Abraham, find ourselves walking along with a downcast gaze, pondering, meditating, trying to reason things out. Nevertheless, *stay in motion*. Keep rolling along in the direction the Lord has pointed you.

Let us settle it in our soul: God has a high purpose for each of us, and the only pathway to fulfilling that purpose comes through *obedience*. Our Father's directives—even when they make no earthly sense to us—are never arbitrary or whimsical. His heart's desire is for us to know *Him* so well that we obey and follow even when we have no clear understanding of what He is doing.

LEARN TO KNOW HIS VOICE

We often raise the question, "But how can I be sure it's the Lord's voice I'm hearing?"

One of the soundest ways to pursue this, if you belong to a Bible-teaching congregation, is to approach one or more of the elders or godly older believers in your fellowship. There ought to be Spirit-led men and women in the church you attend (whether they have a title or not) who, in accordance with the Word of God, are men and women of perception and understanding. Go to one of them and say, "Brother, Sister, I need your help. I need your perspective on this situation." It's wise and practical to seek out those who have walked with Christ for years and submit the matter you are uncertain about to them. Their caution or confirmation can be helpful, and as time goes along, you will gain a deeper confidence in your perception of the Lord's voice as you benefit from the wisdom of others.

Remember, Abraham had been walking with the Lord and listening to His voice for decades before he marched out in obedience toward Moriah. He was not the kind of person who gets some harebrained idea in his head because it seems spiritual and goes streaking across the sky like a meteorite, only to fade in a silent fizzle. He was a man who knew the voice of his Lord.

We, too, can learn to know that voice and then move ahead with the same measure of confidence that Abraham experienced. That confidence in God's trustworthiness sustained him in the face of a command that must have felt like walking straight into a wall of flame.

As the Lord called Abraham to do something that had never been a part of His ways, Abraham moved on in obedience, possessed by the certainty of two things. First, God had clearly said to him, "*In Isaac* your seed shall be called" (Genesis 21:12). Second, He had also told him that his descendants would be as numerous as the sand of the seashore and the stars of the sky.

Yet, now God was saying, "Sacrifice *that* child."

With his obedient response to this directive, Abraham revealed a willingness to lay down Isaac—the very one who God had specifically said would be the fulfillment of His purpose in Abraham's life. This was *the one*. In effect, then, Abraham was being asked to lay on the altar all of God's promises to him—to trust God with life itself.

In the last chapter we discussed our common tendency to protect ourselves. Here in Genesis 22, we meet Abraham at a cliff-edge of faith and surrender beyond anything he had experienced to that point in life. As we stand with him on that sheer cliff, we too may learn to say, "Lord, You have given me exactly that for which I have yearned and hungered for years on end. But I am willing to trust You with that too; I'm willing to lay it before You, Lord, in sacrifice."

As I meditated on these verses, I felt especially prompted to speak a serious word to young men and women in my own congregation, ones who were involved in dating relationships. In the context of this passage, I told them, "You may be falling in love with someone and feel you are moving in God's will. But let me caution you: You need to keep that person completely on the altar before the Lord until the day you repeat your wedding vows to one another. I believe this is a point of wisdom the Lord taught me when I was a young man, looking forward to marrying Anna.

"As ridiculous as it sounds, after more than a year and a half of going steady with her, looking toward our marriage with deep excitement and anticipation, I came up to the last week before the wedding still saying, 'Lord, I really feel confident of Your direction here, and You know how much I love this girl. But I am trusting You to stop this wedding, to somehow break this off if this is not Your best and highest purpose for Anna and me. Lord, I leave it in Your hands.

"I believe with all my heart that one of the reasons there has been such fulfillment in our married life and family life through the years is because the relationship was on the altar all the way down the trail. When we finally stood before the Lord at the marriage altar, we had a deep confidence of God's pleasure and the *rightness* of our union. And for any relationship to develop in the will of God, there must be an open-handedness before the Lord, a continual willingness before Him to do whatever He says, even if it hurts very deeply."

What has the Lord given you? He provides us all with marvelous things: love, blessings, provision. But each of us needs to remain open, trusting, always ready to submit those things to His Lordship, acknowledging, "Lord, it *all* belongs to You. I trust You in everything."

Let me add one more thought: One of the most detestable things the devil does is somehow convince people that if God ever asks anything of them, it's because He doesn't want them to be happy; that He wants them to end up on the short end of life. It happens to be a very old lie—dating back to Eden—a lie that if we're seduced to believe it, will warp and shrivel our lives.

God's great heart of love and intended blessing for you and me is *fixed* on our interests. "'For I know the plans I have for you,' declares the LORD, 'plans to prosper you and not to harm you, plans to give you hope and a future'" (Jeremiah 29:11, NIV). His nature doesn't change: "I am the LORD, I do not change" (Malachi 3:6). "Jesus Christ is the same yesterday, today, and forever" (Hebrews 13:8). "He remembers his covenant forever,...for a thousand generations" (1 Chronicles 16:15, NIV).

Rest in these revelations of His unswerving way: God loves *you*. He sent His only Son to die for *you*, to redeem *you*. He sent His Holy Spirit to be *your* Counselor, *your* Companion, *your* Guide through all your days. It's *your* best He desires. Those things are true and will *always* be true.

Settle it in your heart: He will never, never change.

STOP TRYING TO FIGURE GOD OUT

Abraham's answer to God's call in this episode with Isaac is a lesson that calls us to wean the word *why* from our lips. The fact is, we don't *need* to know why things turn out the way they do. We don't *need* all of our questions answered on demand.

Even so, none of us defers to the Lord's understanding easily! In my own pursuit of God's will, I've found the following passage decisively helpful—worth memorizing and repeating frequently!

> "For My thoughts are not your thoughts, nor are your ways My ways," says the LORD. "For as the heavens are higher than the earth, so are My ways higher than your ways, and My thoughts than your thoughts." (Isaiah 55:8–9)

Somewhere along the line we each need to concede the probability that God has just a few more effectively functioning mental processes than we've got! God wants us to be willing to say, "Lord, I'm not really going to try to understand what's happening. I can't attempt to process this through my limited comprehension—at least at this time. So believing Your wisdom and ways exceed my grasp until You grant me the advantage of higher insight or hindsight, I now put it all in Your hands. I'm satisfied to rest it there."

That *is* the beginning of understanding His ways. When I cease trying to pin God down to a patched-together logic system of my own construction, I've made real headway in my walk with Him.

So it was that this man who launched out to sacrifice his son, burdened with *apparent* evidence that God had changed, learned the *absolute* evidence of His changelessness.

It's a truth that made all the difference to Abraham—as it does to us.

WHERE OUR SECURITY LIES

Abraham was gripped by an assurance that was greater than the grip of horror and sorrow he felt at the prospect of slaying his own son. His feelings of vulnerability and fear over this situation were overwhelmed by the familiarity and certainty of *knowing God Himself.*

Imagine this dialog:

> "Go! Sacrifice your son on a mountain I will show you."
>
> "Yes, Lord, but before I leave, could You at least specify the place?"

But no—that interaction did not occur. Why? Because Abraham had begun this walk with God by going out without knowing, and he was content to continue. And, dear one, that's the way it will continue for us as well, until the Lord brings us all Home.

The fact is, you and I will never find security as the world defines it. In our pursuit of the will of God, security lies in something more—in *Someone* whose rock-solid, changeless nature is committed to support and sustain us by the same eternal love, grace, and power that has saved and forgiven us. Sing it out with the psalmist:

> God is our refuge and strength,
> A very present help in trouble.
> Therefore we will not fear,
> Though the earth be removed,
> And though the mountains be carried into the midst of the sea;
> Though its waters roar and be troubled,
> Though the mountains shake with its swelling.
> There is a river whose streams shall make glad the city of God,
> The holy place of the tabernacle of the Most High.
> God is in the midst of her, she shall not be moved.
>
> (Psalm 46:1–5)

Such a place of settled confidence secured Abraham.

Imagine yet another dialog:

> Abraham (to the young men accompanying him and Isaac): "Stay here with the donkey. The lad and I will go yonder and worship, *and we will come back to you.*"
>
> "Abraham, how do you know that?"
>
> "Because God told me my descendants would come through Isaac, and so whatever occurs, Isaac shall return with me. Alive."

"But, Abraham, hasn't God commanded you to *kill* Isaac? How then could the promise possibly be fulfilled?"

"Yes, I know. I am to sacrifice Isaac. But what God says now will not violate what He said before. His word to me is *one:* In *Isaac* my seed is going to be called."

"How can a dead child produce living offspring?"

"That's God's responsibility. Mine is only to obey. The Eternal One, the Most High, is mighty enough even to raise Isaac from the dead [see Hebrews 11:17–19]. So I tell you this: We will be coming back, Isaac and I. *Together.*"

We all know the rest of the story, revealing the crowning evidence of Abraham's absolute confidence in God's promise to him. But as we read and receive its poignant conclusion—

Isaac's question: "Where is the lamb, my father?"
Abraham's reply: "The Lord will provide, my son."
God's intervention: "Abraham, Abraham, do not harm the boy!"

—we come to one majestic discovery and one grand conclusion.

In his faithful obedience, Abraham was ushered into the secrets of God's counsel and the very heart of God's plan for human redemption. Abraham's words *after* the ram was substituted as a sacrifice in Isaac's place indicate a flash of revelation dawning over the old patriarch's soul.

"Jehovah-jireh!" he declares. "The LORD Will Provide."

But it was more than a name he learned that day on the stark hilltop. He added, "In the Mount of the LORD *it shall be provided.*"

Do you hear the future announced in those words? Do you hear the ring of prophecy?

You see, loved one, Abraham's pursuit of God's will not only brought him to a place of seeing God's provision, it brought him into a place of understanding

God's counsel and plans. It's the highest place we can know in our walk with God. No, it doesn't mean we have become omniscient or have some kind of inside track on all that God does. Not at all. Nevertheless, Scripture gives us this amazing—if mysterious—assurance: "The secret of the LORD is with those who fear Him, and He will show them His covenant" (Psalm 25:14).

This, then, is the majestic discovery: a glimpse into the very heart of God, an unfolding of His secrets to those who will become wholly His own.

But there is also a grand conclusion to be drawn.

As Abraham went all the way to the utmost limit in his obedience—ready to plunge the knife into the chest of his beloved son—he discovered the great fact that however delayed God's answers are, He is never late. To pursue God's will for a lifetime is to learn the richest realities of God's nature and to have them become rooted in the deepest dimensions of His love.

The call to leave Ur and the call to sacrifice Isaac were drastically different in the degree of faith each required. But in between, the man called Abraham had a lifetime of growth in the privilege of pursuing God's will.

The result of that journey was threefold:

He received God's promises.
He learned God's heart.
He became an instrument of blessing in God's hands.

And the results will be the same today whenever any of us will answer the Holy Spirit's call to pursue the will of God in Christ our Lord. Count the threefold results above, and know they await you too.

Follow on!

RESOURCES FOR PURSUING THE WILL OF GOD

Book:

Reflections and Meditations on the Life of Abraham

Pastor Jack Hayford presents timeless, biblical principals that teach believers how to discern, pursue, and walk in God's will.

PTWG02 Pursuing the Will of God

Audio Series:

A Study in the Life of Abraham

Pastor Jack Hayford presents practical principles which will equip and nurture a holy pursuit for the will of God in each believer's life.

PWG Principles of Pursuing the Will of God
11 tape audio series

Mini Album:

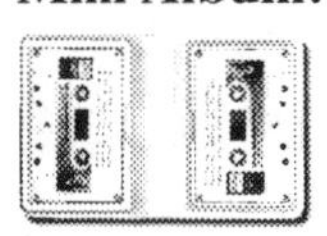

The Will of God Series

4330 To Pour a Little Heaven on Your World
4332 To Grow a Little Heaven in Your World

Individual Tapes:

Keeping In and Out of God's Way

3302	Pt.1: Keeping In	3305	Pt.2: Keeping Out
15	Knowing God's Will Pt.1	16	Knowing God's Will Pt.2
1078	God's Will for Us	1591	The Human Quest for the Divine Will
3656	The Will of God	4232	Your "Aegis" and God's Will

For additional copies of these cassette tapes and more resources, please contact:

Living Way Ministries®

CALL 1-800-776-8180 www.livingway.org

Related Ministries of Pastor Jack Hayford

THE KING'S COLLEGE AND SEMINARY

The King's College and Seminary are preparing leaders for the 21st century with education at its best. For more information about earning your Bachelor's Degree from the The King's College, call toll free 1-888-779-8040 or visit www.kingscollege.edu. For information about earning a Master's Degree from the King's Seminary, call toll free 1-877-HAYFORD or visit www.kingsseminary.edu.

LIVING WAY MINISTRIES

Living Way Ministries serves to develop and distribute the messages, books, tapes, and other resources from the respected teaching ministry of Pastor Jack Hayford. Our radio and television programs can be heard/seen around the world, and found on our web site at www.livingway.org. You may also listen "live" to our radio station, KTLW, online at www.ktlw.net.

THE CHURCH ON THE WAY

Pastor Jack Hayford continues to serve the congregation of The Church On The Way in Van Nuys, California as its Founding Pastor and Minister at Large. He serves beside TCOTW's Senior Pastor, Scott Bauer, as a key associate while continuing his travel ministry and role as the Chancellor and President of The King's Seminary. For more information on the church's current ministry visit www.tcotw.org.

THE JACK W. HAYFORD SCHOOL OF PASTORAL NURTURE

This special "leadership advancement program" is focused on increasing ministry effectiveness of pastors and leaders by facilitating personal growth and renewal. Join a small group of 35-45 pastors and spend an intensive week with Pastor Jack Hayford in disciplined reflection and interaction. Visit www.kingsseminary.edu.

The Hayford Files

This unique online format is designed to provide ministry resources and support for pastors and leaders, and to reinforce leadership principles taught at the Jack W. Hayford School of Pastoral Nurture. Subscribers will have access to an extensive and growing library of Pastor Hayford's sermon outlines with suggested worship songs, teachings on worship and deliverance, and "practical pastoring" articles, as well as an international pastor-to-pastor forum. For more information visit www.jackhayford.com or call 1-818-779-8550.

JackHayford.com

Enter a new frontier with jackhayford.com: providing relevant, edifying, and useful content to the Church and the community, with a special emphasis on ministry to pastors and leaders. Find online links to resources and related ministries.